MW00466122

To Yota : Dan —

May your future be
filled with many positive breakthroughs!

THE BREAKTHROUGH MANIFESTO

THE BREAKTHROUGH MANIFESTO

10 PRINCIPLES TO SPARK TRANSFORMATIVE INNOVATION

KIM CHRISTFORT
SUZANNE VICKBERG

WILEY

Copyright © 2024 by John Wiley & Sons, Inc. All rights reserved.

Published by John Wiley & Sons, Inc., Hoboken, New Jersey.
Published simultaneously in Canada.

No part of this publication may be reproduced, stored in a retrieval system, or transmitted in any form or by any means, electronic, mechanical, photocopying, recording, scanning, or otherwise, except as permitted under Section 107 or 108 of the 1976 United States Copyright Act, without either the prior written permission of the Publisher, or authorization through payment of the appropriate per-copy fee to the Copyright Clearance Center, Inc., 222 Rosewood Drive, Danvers, MA 01923, (978) 750-8400, fax (978) 750-4470, or on the web at www.copyright.com. Requests to the Publisher for permission should be addressed to the Permissions Department, John Wiley & Sons, Inc., 111 River Street, Hoboken, NJ 07030, (201) 748-6011, fax (201) 748-6008, or online at http://www.wiley.com/go/permission.

Trademarks: Wiley and the Wiley logo are trademarks or registered trademarks of John Wiley & Sons, Inc. and/or its affiliates in the United States and other countries and may not be used without written permission. All other trademarks are the property of their respective owners. John Wiley & Sons, Inc. is not associated with any product or vendor mentioned in this book.

Limit of Liability/Disclaimer of Warranty: While the publisher and author have used their best efforts in preparing this book, they make no representations or warranties with respect to the accuracy or completeness of the contents of this book and specifically disclaim any implied warranties of merchantability or fitness for a particular purpose. No warranty may be created or extended by sales representatives or written sales materials. The advice and strategies contained herein may not be suitable for your situation. You should consult with a professional where appropriate. Further, readers should be aware that websites listed in this work may have changed or disappeared between when this work was written and when it is read. Neither the publisher nor authors shall be liable for any loss of profit or any other commercial damages, including but not limited to special, incidental, consequential, or other damages.

For general information on our other products and services or for technical support, please contact our Customer Care Department within the United States at (800) 762-2974, outside the United States at (317) 572-3993 or fax (317) 572-4002.

Wiley also publishes its books in a variety of electronic formats. Some content that appears in print may not be available in electronic formats. For more information about Wiley products, visit our web site at www.wiley.com.

Library of Congress Cataloging-in-Publication Data

Names: Christfort, Kim, 1974- author. | Vickberg, Suzanne, 1971-, author. | John Wiley & Sons, publisher.
Title: The breakthrough manifesto : 10 principles to spark transformative innovation / Kim Christfort, Suzanne Vickberg.
Description: Hoboken, New Jersey : Wiley, [2024] | Includes bibliographical references and index.
Identifiers: LCCN 2023026401 (print) | LCCN 2023026402 (ebook) | ISBN 9781394207039 (cloth) | ISBN 9781394207053 (adobe pdf) | ISBN 9781394207046 (epub)
Subjects: LCSH: Organizational change—Management.
Classification: LCC HD58.8 .C487 2024 (print) | LCC HD58.8 (ebook) | DDC 658.4/06—dc23/eng/20230905
LC record available at https://lccn.loc.gov/2023026401
LC ebook record available at https://lccn.loc.gov/2023026402

Cover Design and Image: Emily Hung Wilson

To our motley Deloitte Greenhouse crew and alumni, who have been the inspiration and the engine behind this book

Contents

Welcome to Breakthrough

We believe in breakthrough. Not so much the random unicorn kind that might meander across your path (though we're all for that). But even more so the hard-earned variety that comes when you open your mind, dig deep, and lean in. The type that requires you to embrace and to rise above your humanness.

But what is breakthrough, really?

Breakthrough is what enables people to create better versions of themselves and the world around them. It is the array of energizing injection points on the timeline of progress and the catalyst of step change transformations. Breakthrough is a way of thinking that opens eyes to new possibilities and a way of acting that converts that potential into impact.

History is replete with stories, perhaps exaggerated, about sudden moments of inspired breakthrough. Newton's insight into gravity after an apple fell on his head. Einstein's dream of a falling man inspiring the theory of relativity. Archimedes's naked run through the streets shouting "Eureka" after he made the connection between mass and water displacement while in his tub.

These scientific discoveries are certainly one type of breakthrough. But what about the stories of challenges overcome in defiance of the standard? For instance, the design school team who took on the challenge of infant survival rates in low resource environments by building a baby warmer that costs less than 1% that of a traditional incubator.[1] Or any of the "miracle" athletic wins, when records are shattered and context overcome, like two-time Olympic gold medalist Sydney McLaughlin, who broke her own world record in the 400-meter hurdles four times in a 13-month period. These, too, are types of breakthrough.

Over the past decade working with thousands of executives and their teams in immersive Deloitte Greenhouse® experiences, we've witnessed these kinds of breakthroughs with many moments of sudden inspiration and numerous challenges overcome. But we see another kind of breakthrough as well, unique in that it stems not from an obligation to address a specific existing problem but rather a desire to anticipate and act on emerging issues and needs. This is breakthrough that happens when people decide to step outside the comfort of the status quo to ask, "What if . . . ?," enabling new opportunities to blink into existence and eventually take flight.

This sort of breakthrough is essential, particularly in this current moment. Around the world foundational beliefs and behaviors are shifting rapidly and simultaneously across societal, political, and economic arenas. Rapid advances in technology are driving entirely new worlds of opportunity with the potential for great benefit but also great harm.[2] Traditional optimization and innovation approaches can fall short in this environment. Instead, organizations need a different way of thinking that helps to imagine and shape the future and effect transformational change.

At their core, each of these breakthrough definitions shares a dramatic shift from *before* to *after*. And although breakthrough with widespread implications might be the kind making news headlines, we've also seen that breakthrough can be highly personal. That fear you had that you overcame. That realization you had that transformed your thinking. Moments of accomplishment or insight that might not have changed *the* world, but that changed *your* world. Because breakthrough ultimately is about significant positive change—period.

We think of breakthrough in terms of its two central aspects, inherent in the name:

• **BREAK** – obliterating barriers and obstacles that stand between you and the place you're trying to get to on the other side

• **THROUGH** – not just leaving things broken, but rather creating momentum to successfully transition between the *from* and the *to*

To achieve breakthrough, you must first realize that there's a problem or opportunity relative to your current state. Then, you must figure out what's getting in the way and how to deal with that, and you must build the impetus and drive to achieve the desired change. Breakthrough is process and product, and the journey to breakthrough can be as significant as the destination itself, because you rarely get the latter without the former.

In spite of its importance and impact, we've found that the process of getting to breakthrough isn't standard fare for most individuals and teams. It requires a certain type of mindset and thinking that spurs you to engage with the world differently. After years of research and working with executives in the field, we have found that there are specific principles and techniques that, when applied with intention and regularity, can enhance your chances of getting to breakthrough. And that is what this book is all about.

The 10 Breakthrough Manifesto Principles

PRINCIPLE 1:
Silence your cynic

Suspend disbelief and assume anything's possible.

PRINCIPLE 2:
Strip away everything

Question your assumptions and adopt a beginner's mindset.

PRINCIPLE 3:
Live with the problem

Invest time in understanding a problem deeply before attempting to solve it.

PRINCIPLE 4:
Check your edge

Push your thinking and ask whether your ideas are truly innovative or unique.

PRINCIPLE 5:
Enlist a motley crew

Seek unusual perspectives on a problem, from beyond your own team or "usual suspects."

PRINCIPLE 6:
Get real

Get vulnerable with each other and share your whole, authentic selves.

PRINCIPLE 7:
Make a mess

Try something out or create a prototype rather than just talking about hypotheses or possible solutions.

PRINCIPLE 8:
Don't play "nice"

Speak the truth and call out the elephants in the room.

PRINCIPLE 9:
Dial up the drama

Use storytelling or other ways to engage emotions and senses as you solve a problem.

PRINCIPLE 10:
Make change

Champion change, embrace flexibility, and always keep evolving.

Copyright © 2023 Deloitte Development LLC. All rights reserved.

Based on more than a decade of work with individuals, teams, and organizations, the Breakthrough Manifesto codifies 10 principles that underpin everything we do in the Deloitte Greenhouse to help our clients and ourselves achieve breakthrough.

This two-part book brings the Breakthrough Manifesto to life with research, behavioral science, stories from the field, and practical strategies. It addresses why these principles are needed and why they work, and it offers pragmatic, straightforward methods for implementing this way of thinking in day-to-day life to effect positive change.

Because these principles are core to what we do in the Deloitte Greenhouse, it's perhaps not surprising that this is a business book, based on years of business experience and research, written for business practitioners and their teams. That said, similar to many human-centered insights, our findings and recommendations for breakthrough thinking can apply beyond the work domain. And similar to many such insights, the more you build your breakthrough thinking muscles in one domain, the more you might find those muscles flexing in other aspects of your life. So, in that spirit, although much of this book focuses on workplace examples, we will also call out specific personal applications in each chapter and hope you'll be inspired to think of others on your own.

After reading this list of principles you may think that you are already doing many of these things. Indeed, we asked 9,500 professionals from more than 1,000 companies around the world whether they're living these principles, and the majority said they are—different principles to differing degrees. And yet, those same professionals also shared that they don't believe their teams embrace the principles to the same extent. Because teams (who apparently aren't embracing the principles) are made up of individuals (who claim they are), someone must be over- or underestimating some behaviors somewhere.

Although this difference in perception of one's own versus others' behaviors likely stems from a shared superiority illusion[3] (whereby people tend to think they, individually, perform above average in a variety of different ways), our research does show differences in perceived "breakthrough mindedness" based on working style, industry, and even maturity of a team (e.g., short-term project teams claim to use more of the principles, and more permanent teams representing a department or division use fewer). And there are also differences in degree of adoption for some principles compared to others, with the largest proportion of professionals claiming they're *making change*, and the smallest proportion claim they're *getting real* or *checking their edge*. Overall, however, we've seen that although many people and teams have good intentions, they often don't incorporate breakthrough thinking into their day to day lives. They lack daily habits and practices to build muscle memory for catalyzing and promoting innovation. And although that may not pose a challenge for some efforts, when it comes to promoting innovation that effects significant positive transformation—real breakthrough—ad hoc approaches fall short.

That's why this book doesn't just explain the different principles behind the Breakthrough Manifesto but also offers specific methods for how to create breakthrough-friendly environments, prime your brain for breakthrough thinking, spark breakthrough ideas, and generate momentum to bring breakthroughs to life. Each chapter in Part 1 explores one of the 10 principles, and then the corresponding sections in Part 2 provide a field guide of related methods for you to try on your own or with your teams to boost your breakthrough thinking. It's designed to be a resource that you actively use in your daily life, versus browse and tuck away on a shelf. These methods can serve as a starting point for you to add to and annotate with your own breakthrough ideas as you experiment on your own. And experiment we hope you will.

It won't always be easy. Breakthrough isn't for the faint of heart. It requires bravery, authenticity, and sweat. Throughout the process you'll be asking yourself and others to think differently, share openly, and act boldly—practices that require cognitive agility, psychological safety, perceived value and impact, and healthy group dynamics, among other things. Throughout the book we'll share tips for how to overcome potential barriers and create environments that promote breakthrough thinking.

At the end of the day, we believe the effort is worth it. Improving your breakthrough thinking enables you to broaden horizons, unlock stale thinking, and seed fresh ideas, creating paths to meaningful impact at scale. And we suspect you'll find, as have we, that it's not just about reaching a specific destination; even the journey itself makes a difference.

Our Barriers to Breakthrough Study

Although a lack of psychological safety has been well-established as a barrier to breakthrough, it's not the only thing that keeps people from bringing their best to team discussions, brainstorming sessions, and creative problem-solving efforts.[4] Our `Barriers to Breakthrough` study was designed to uncover what else gets in the way.

Between 2019 and 2021 we surveyed 28,000 professionals working in hundreds of organizations around the world and across a variety of industries, from C-suite leaders to junior staff members.[5] We found a wide variety of conditions can discourage contribution, from distraction to disinterest to doubt about the value of one's own offerings.

Throughout the book, when you see a reference to `Barriers to Breakthrough` this is the study we're referring to.

SILENCE YOUR CYNIC
Suspend disbelief and assume everything's possible.
No great breakthrough was born of a naysayer.

Copyright © 2023 Deloitte Development LLC. All rights reserved.

CHAPTER
01

In many ways, these are mistrusting times. Fake news, scams, and hoaxes have littered the past decade. So perhaps it's not only understandable, but even healthy, to maintain a general air of skepticism. To doubt. To question. To dismiss. Some might even view such behavior as a sign of intelligence; poking holes in things can seem insightful whereas postulating possibilities can come across as naive.[6] Indeed, research suggests that people often perceive skeptics to be cognitively superior. This despite studies demonstrating precisely the opposite.[7] It's no wonder then that the skeptic can have such a powerful voice in our world and in our workplace.

But although healthy skepticism plays an essential role in effective evaluation and decision-making, cynicism, its negative cousin, can be toxic. Perhaps you've seen this less desirable orientation play out in your teams or organization. The blunt naysayer shutting down discussion with a dismissive, "That will never work." The snide Goldilocks sidebar chats undermining an idea for being too much, or too little, but never just right. Or perhaps even that critical narrative in your own head whispering, "There's no way you can do this." Unfortunately, this kind of negativity can be contagious and counterproductive, particularly for breakthrough thinking.

At this point you may be wondering (with, we might add, healthy skepticism), "Now wait a second, am I just supposed to stop thinking critically and not say anything, no matter how ridiculous the situation? The answer is no. Indeed, in order to get to breakthrough it is essential that you apply keen reasoning and judgment, speak up to question assumptions, and share your perspectives. It's just a question of when and how. *Silence your cynic* is about making room for ideas to take shape and germinate. It's about suspending disbelief and assuming anything's possible. Our other Breakthrough Principles get into how you can prune those ideas later.

As you will see throughout this guide, the 10 principles of our Breakthrough Manifesto are designed to work in combination, but they don't need to be used all together, or at the same time. This way of thinking requires agility to apply the principles in specific moments to increase your probability of getting to breakthrough. And it's hard to get to breakthrough if you don't at least start with an open mind. That's why straight out of the gate we clear the path for breakthrough by tackling the toxic effects of cynicism head on. If you look closely, you'll see cynicism can result in death to innovation, saying bye-bye to diversity, and placing shackles on the mind.

Stories from the Field

Silence Your Cynic

An executive asked us for help solving the mystery of what was holding her team back. She bemoaned their lack of innovation and had "tried everything," by her accounting, to get them to come up with fresh ideas, but no luck. They were reluctant to contribute anything at all, and what they did offer was less than innovative. She just didn't get it.

At the start of a brainstorming session, she told her team to think of her as a mother lion who would protect them from threats so they could achieve great things, and the team seemed somewhat encouraged. But no sooner did they voice their first idea than the executive pounced on them with a series of cynical questions, each one seeming to interrogate the quality of their thinking and allege their lack of ingenuity. Instantly the positive energy and confidence crumbled. The conversation became stilted and rote, and no one was willing to speak up.

The lioness had betrayed her cubs, and why this team struggled to innovate was a mystery no more.

Toxic Effect 1: Death to Innovation

Did you ever hear that story about the amazing idea that was dismissed too quickly and thus never changed the world? Right. Breakthroughs are more likely to arise in open environments where ideation produces a high volume and diversity of ideas.[8] Especially in the initial stages of idea development, it's essential to create a positive, unconstrained environment that encourages imaginative meanderings, random associations, and outlandish what-ifs so you can move beyond the obvious ideas to the truly creative ones. Being overly critical too early in the process isn't just a buzzkill, it can be a barrier to discovering and unlocking new opportunity spaces.

Some organizations send their executives to improvisation classes, and there's a good reason for that. The classic "Yes, and . . ." technique encourages people to build off one another's ideas, however ridiculous, rather than shutting them down with a "No" or "That doesn't make sense" or "What the heck are you thinking?" It may seem like fun and games but following a seemingly bizarre thought can lead down a path to a related idea that works.

Part of the power of a new idea is that, by definition, it hasn't been done before. Yet innovation can be nipped in the bud because it challenges the status quo or seems at first glance inferior to it. The internet is bursting with stories about inventions that experts said would never be *a thing*: lightbulbs, alternating current, telephones, cars, planes, personal computers, online shopping, books about boy wizards, and so on! These examples illustrate how an unwavering belief in their own idea can enable creators to ignore the cynics who doubt them. It can be inspiring to read these *believe in yourself* stories, but you shouldn't let them fool you about the potentially destructive effects of judgment and cynicism. In that moment of a possible breakthrough's birth, and without the benefit of hindsight, the cynical voice can drown out future potential with vociferous defense of the present. And thus is the status quo calcified and opportunity lost.

One of our favorite examples of how a seemingly random idea can lead to genius notions is the story of a team who was struggling with how to keep ice-coated power lines from breaking. Their existing solution was suboptimal, requiring humans to climb up power line poles and manually shake the ice off, an arduous and dangerous process. The group decided to brainstorm alternative solutions. During the ideation an idea was jokingly surfaced that perhaps the problem could be solved by training bears to climb up the poles instead of humans.

Ha, yes! And . . . maybe we could put pots of honey on the top of the poles to lure the bears up. Yes! And . . . maybe helicopters could be used to place the pots of honey, ha! Wait a minute. Maybe helicopters could be used . . .

The eventual solution they reached was to fly helicopters near to the power lines, so that the vibrations from the helicopter blades would shake the ice off.[9] And that's how you get from bears to breakthrough.

Barriers to Breakthrough

44% of the people we surveyed indicated they may withhold their ideas if they fear someone will shoot them down.

41% said a discussion focused on why ideas won't work might discourage their contributions.

An idea can be like an offering, and when people anticipate it may be rejected, they may not offer it in the first place. **Silencing your cynic,** even just in the beginning stages of brainstorming, can help get more ideas on the table.

Toxic Effect 2: Bye, Bye Diverse Ideas

As we've shared, innovation thrives on quantity and diversity of ideas. This comes not only through promoting free-ranging discussions that push beyond the status quo but also through establishing psychologically safe environments that encourage broad participation. As we'll explore further in the *enlist a motley crew* chapter, there is often enormous benefit to accessing and engaging multiple perspectives. Diversity of all sorts can be a key factor in generating more creative solutions.[10] Yet this diversity often isn't tapped, even when it exists on a team or in an organization. Why not? Because according to our research, many people feel they can't share their ideas freely at work due to fear of judgment and rejection.[11]

Not surprisingly, leaders have an outsized influence on their team's willingness to voice their thoughts. Sometimes teams withhold critical information, or stop sharing fresh perspectives, because their leaders respond with whiplash cynicism and negativity. These teams may share a common set of sentiments, feel attacked, ridiculed, undermined, and mistrusted by the way their leaders respond. But leaders aren't the only source of such problems. If any team member voices cynicism, it can catalyze a cascade of naysaying that only exacerbates the issue.

In many instances, *what* the cynics say isn't the problem. Asking difficult questions and exercising good judgment are essential to effective leadership and management. Often the issue is with the *when*, the *why*, and the *how*.

Take for example two leaders soliciting input from their teams. One asks for opinions, and then the moment an individual shares a point of view, jumps on it and starts picking it apart, saying things like, "That's not at all what that means" and "I don't see any evidence to support that." We call this a *gotcha leader*. The other leader requests opinions and then asks clarifying questions, saying things like, "What do you mean when you say *x*?" and "Interesting; what led you to make that connection?" We call this a *Socratic leader*.

Both types of leaders have questions about the information being provided. In the *gotcha leader* example, the team member who spoke up likely feels interrogated and might be reluctant to share anything more for fear of further criticism. That person's teammates are probably happy that *they* aren't the ones in the line of fire and might be scrupulously avoiding eye contact with the leader in the hopes of not being attacked themselves. In the *Socratic leader* example, the team member who spoke up likely feels heard. The neutral questions enable the person to share more of their thoughts and underlying assumptions, yielding better information. And their teammates are able to listen and react to their ideas and are more likely to be willing to share their own. Using inquiry as a thoughtful tool to create a safe environment for diverse contributions is a critical component of breakthrough thinking.

THE WHEN

Early ideas are like fresh shoots—easily destroyed by a cold breeze or careless tread. Similarly, a person speaking up for the first time, two individuals establishing a new relationship, or a group dealing with a situation they've never before faced may be particularly susceptible to cynicism. This is especially true for people who tend to be more introverted or risk averse.[12] Judgment delivered early in a relationship, before trust has been established, or early in the generation of an idea, can be particularly damaging and can discourage people from contributing to the breakthrough process.

THE WHY

There are many reasons one may be skeptical, but some of the more damaging reasons to voice that skepticism relate to power and politics. Is that idea really bad, or does it support an opinion I don't back? Is that line of thinking drawing into question my own expertise and knowledge on this topic? Does it contradict a decision I've made in the past? People can be more likely to lean into cynicism when they're feeling vulnerable.[13] Using cynicism and doubt as a shield for one's own insecurity not only quells others' desire to engage but also it closes off one's own mind to potentially revelatory perspectives.

THE HOW

The means by which skepticism is voiced and satisfied is another critical aspect of its reception. Is the doubt voiced as a question or as a statement? Is the tone of voice curious or accusatory? Is the skepticism raised one-on-one, or in front of others where personal reputation may be at stake? It is essential to stress again that skepticism can be healthy, and that often a vocal skeptic is trying to do something right. But to encourage people to contribute, the devil can be in the delivery.

Toxic Effect 3: Shackles on the Mind

Perhaps the most insidious type of cynicism is the type aimed not at others, but at oneself. The inner voice saying, "I can't," "That's impossible," "I'm not [insert positive adjective] enough." Ironically, that voice is likely even louder when there's *another* cynic around, perhaps someone like the *gotcha leader* criticizing ideas, or even a colleague snarkily judging other individuals on the team. An inner cynic may see that kind of behavior and sow even more self-doubt.

Even without external cynicism to strengthen it, the inner cynic can be quite chatty—especially when it comes to breakthrough thinking. It can feel personally risky to explore half-baked, potentially unpopular, ambitious thoughts. That process reveals a bit of yourself in *how* you think and *what* you think about and may even require bold things *of* you.

But a negative inner monologue can become a self-fulfilling prophesy. It's difficult to get to breakthrough if you doubt you're capable of reaching it. Indeed, belief in oneself has been demonstrated to make people see more opportunities and be more open to risks.[14] Like the Little Engine Who Could, Rocky, Ted Lasso, and countless other popular references, you have to believe it to achieve it.

When you believe, you are "seeing" something that is not yet in sight, that has no "real" evidence for its existence. You are putting your eye on a daring horizon point, even if you don't know precisely how you'll get there, versus fixing your gaze on the obstacles of your current reality. Belief is the feather that gives you the confidence to fly. Just ask Dumbo. Or Henry Ford who famously said, "Whether you believe you can, or believe you can't, you're right."[15]

Silencing your own cynic to believe—in an idea, in others, in yourself—can also open your mind to making new connections because your brain wants things to make sense. If you are cynical about something but you force yourself to *not* be cynical, then you start a different kind of cognitive processing. What could this mean? How might this make sense? What would it take to make this work? Channel the powers of your inner voice toward breakthrough, not barrier making.

Looking for practical ways to boost your breakthrough thinking by *silencing your cynic*? Jump ahead to our *silence your cynic* methods. We'll guide you through the steps to interrogate yourself, ask what if . . .?, change your mind(set), get physical, and buddy up.

Bottom Line Benefits

Silence Your Cynic

UNREALISTIC
NO / IMPOSSIBLE
DIFFICULT / BUSY
EXPENSIVE / BUT...
TIME-CONSUMING
WE DON'T DO THAT
I DON'T THINK SO
CAN'T / WON'T
BE REALISTIC
I WISH

- Encourages volume and diversity of ideas early on in ideation, leading to better ultimate outcomes and previously unseen opportunities

- Establishes psychologically safe environments that encourage broad participation

- Leaves room for provocative ideas that might challenge the status quo

- Stimulates alternative cognitive processing because your brain is forced to make sense of ideas it's initially inclined to reject

Breakthrough YOU

Silence Your Cynic

Ever feel burnt out? You're not alone. One of the notable trends from the COVID-19 pandemic was an increase in burnout across the population.[16] Burnout goes beyond everyday stress—it's a multifaceted exhaustion that's deleterious to health and well-being. Indeed, three main characteristics define a burnout diagnosis: emotional exhaustion, reduced personal efficacy, and . . . that's right . . . **cynicism**.[17]

If you're suffering burnout, you may be more likely to take a negative view of the people and happenings around you and find yourself inclined to be critical and resentful. But leaning into those feelings not only risks the toxic effects of cynicism mentioned in this chapter but also it can make your burnout worse.[18]

So if you notice yourself feeling cynical, take a moment to ask yourself why. Are your reactions demonstrating healthy skepticism merited by the situation? Or are you perhaps suffering from burnout, and letting that cast a pessimistic pall over all you do? Seeking out the root cause of your cynicism can serve as a mini self-breakthrough to help put you on a path to better health and happiness.

We can't give you a quick three-step remedy for cynicism or burnout (or even a five- or 10-step one), but we can offer up a few tips. For one, although your natural inclination may be to assume easing burnout requires subtracting from your schedule, consider whether the key might actually be adding some carefully selected activities that you enjoy or that give you a sense of meaning.[19] Or tackle your cynicism by taking an awe walk— a stroll during which you bring your awareness to your breath and to your surroundings, viewing everything as if you're seeing it for the first time.[20] Experiencing awe can help you feel connected to something larger and more significant than yourself, reduce negative moods, improve happiness, and make you feel more generous. Finally, connectedness and community can serve as antidotes to burnout.[21] Rather than isolating yourself if you're feeling stressed, reach out to colleagues and loved ones to ask for and offer support.

Breakthrough Requires Business *Not* as Usual

Conducting *business as usual* just may be one of the greatest barriers to break-through thinking. It may seem like a perfectly reasonable way to approach problem-solving, but it's unlikely to get you to a breakthrough solution. Each of the Breakthrough Manifesto principles represents a significant departure from a reasonable-sounding business as usual approach.

If you hear your team using any of the following phrases, read the relevant chapter to understand how that approach may be holding you back, and what you stand to gain from adopting a business *not* as usual approach.

IF YOU HEAR . . .	. . . THEN READ
"Be realistic"	Silence your cynic
"We already know the answer"	Strip away everything
"Time is of the essence"	Live with the problem
"It's good enough"	Check your edge
"We should select teammates based on 'fit'"	Enlist a motley crew
"Getting personal isn't professional"	Get real
"We need to get it right the first time"	Make a mess
"Go along to get along"	Don't play "nice"
"Let's stick with the facts"	Dial up the drama
"If it ain't broke, don't fix it"	Make change

Copyright © 2023 Deloitte Development LLC. All rights reserved.

strip away

EVERYTHING

Set aside everything you think you know.
Assumptions, beliefs, and dogma are the enemy.

Copyright © 2023 Deloitte Development LLC. All rights reserved.

CHAPTER

02

When Einstein proposed his theory of special relativity in 1905, he ended a decades-long search for luminiferous ether, which was believed to fill all unoccupied space and to serve as the medium through which electromagnetic waves are transmitted. Physicists of the day were laboring under the Newtonian assumption that all waves require a medium to propagate, just as sound waves require air. Although they spent an untold number of hours searching for the mysterious medium, no one ever found it. (Because it didn't exist!) Just think what progress might have been made on other scientific discoveries if that erroneous assumption had been challenged earlier, and the energy of those scientists was directed elsewhere.

Although it's perhaps easy to look back and think the physicists of the 1800s should have known better, they were far from unique in accepting faulty assumptions as truth. Einstein himself accepted the false assumption that the universe is static rather than expanding, and he created the *cosmological constant* to force his data to fit that assumption (rather than challenging the assumption itself when he discovered his data didn't fit).[22] Modern day science continues to discover previously accepted assumptions that are false. And regular people—us non-scientists—are always making false assumptions as well. For example, people tend to assume having children will make them happy, but later report they are less happy when interacting with their actual children than when doing almost any other activity.[23] Human lives are built on assumptions, and that can wreak havoc on the choices people make.

Just like other parts of life, the workplace is full of assumptions that, unchallenged, can get in the way of breakthrough. When there's a really tough problem to solve, people often focus on what they don't know, without realizing that what they *do* know (or *think* they know) is equally important. Sometimes they get stuck on a single idea they think will define the future or they accept explanations that may not be accurate. People limit their solution generation by starting with certain assumptions that lead them down one path and close off other paths. They fall victim to their usual patterns of thinking and fail to consider different directions. What you think you know can blind you to new possibilities. Instead, we recommend you *strip away everything*—set aside what you think you know, question your assumptions, and adopt a beginner's mindset. Doing so can help to mitigate the limitations imposed by individual biases, organizational orthodoxies, and societal beliefs alike. So check yourself, question orthodoxies, and don't believe everything you hear.

Stories from the Field

Strip Away Everything

We worked with a health care organization that came to the Deloitte Greenhouse for help with their vision. One of the main points of debate centered on how the company should prioritize its investments. The enterprise was massive, with many business units operating in largely independent silos, and it quickly became clear that each unit had its own take on where the organization should focus its resources.

We dug in further to explore not just *where* each unit thought investments should be made, but *why*. This discussion revealed that, without even realizing it, the different units were working under different assumptions on the organizational goals. By making those assumptions explicit, the group was able to have a rich conversation about what really mattered for the organization as a whole. In addition to uncovering misaligned assumptions, they also identified a *shared* assumption that they felt needed to be challenged—the belief that the health care organization's ultimate goal was to help people live as long as possible. Although this might seem like a reasonable assumption, the team ultimately rejected it and reoriented their vision toward a new goal: helping to not just prolong life but to reach the highest possible quality of life. This shift in the organization's vision had a profound impact on not only their investments but also their overall strategy, operations, and orientation toward their mission.

Check Yourself

At the individual level, everyone has beliefs and assumptions about how the world works. And people's brains have any number of ways to keep those beliefs and assumptions in place. We hate to tell you this, but your brain can be a bit lazy. It doesn't want to go to the effort of looking at things in a completely new and novel way every time. Instead, it uses old information, simplifies things, employs shortcuts, and selectively pays attention in ways that enable it to work a bit less hard. Although we're all for saving energy, your brain's cognitive biases may be getting in the way of breakthrough thinking. And to make it worse, your brain doesn't announce what it's doing. It does so quietly, invisibly. That's why cognitive biases are also known as unconscious biases. Although there are *many* biases that can get in your way, there are three in particular that can snag your progress toward breakthrough thinking.

First, the *status quo bias* is a preference for keeping things the same.[24] In other words, doing nothing, changing nothing—not exactly a recipe for breakthrough. If there is a current state of affairs (and there usually is), this bias leads your brain to prefer just going with that, especially if the current state of affairs is the result of a decision that was made in the past. You'll hear quite a bit more about the status quo bias in the chapters to come. For now, suffice to say that *stripping away everything* means challenging your own preference for the status quo.

Second, the *confirmation bias* is another way in which your brain can make it difficult to question your assumptions. This bias leads you to notice, interpret favorably, and remember information that confirms what you already believe, and to ignore, interpret unfavorably, or forget contradicting information.[25] Your brain is working against you triple time with this one. If it comes across information it can't ignore, no problem; it will decide it means something different, or it will simply forget it! When you're trying to break out of an old way of doing things and break through to a new way, your brain often seems to be setting you up to fail so you need to make a very conscious effort to think differently.

Reading the previous two paragraphs has likely already brought you closer to combating the status quo and confirmation biases. It's easier to notice something when you're looking for it—that's the reason for *moose crossing* and *falling rock* signs on potentially treacherous sections of road—and being aware that these biases exist can help you spot them more easily. When you're working on a problem that needs a breakthrough solution, ask yourself whether you're falling victim to these biases. Then, challenge them directly. Ask questions such as, "Are the way things are really the way they *have* to be?" Or "What information might I be missing, forgetting, or interpreting through a biased lens?" Because cognitive biases happen in our individual brains, it can be particularly helpful to work together to surface them, so don't stop at asking yourself those questions; ask them of others as well.

The third bias might be particularly challenging to root out if you're an experienced professional who has spent years honing your craft, and/or if your colleagues and leaders are highly knowledgeable. Being a smart person working with other smart people is the dream, right? Knowledge can be valuable, no question, but when it comes to problem-solving, it can also get in your way. The *earned dogmatism effect* describes a phenomenon that occurs when someone is labeled an expert—they tend to become more closed-minded.[26] This effect is so strong that it can happen even if someone isn't *actually* an expert, but they've been asked to play the expert in an experiment. And when solving a tough problem, being closed-minded isn't to your benefit, especially because what you "know" is sometimes wrong.

Barriers to Breakthrough

88% of the people we surveyed suggested they'd be less likely to contribute thoughts, questions, or ideas if they had nothing valuable to add to a discussion.

On the one hand that seems reasonable, even preferable, but how are people defining "valuable"?

89% indicated they'd hesitate to share if they don't have enough background information or data, **83%** if they don't know much about the issue, and **52%** if someone else who's present is an expert.

A beginner's mindset can bring fresh approaches. Encouraging team members to **strip away** their assumptions about what makes for a valuable contribution could get more varied and innovative ideas into the mix.

Instead, adopting a beginner's mindset can be a better path to identifying truly innovative ideas. That means putting aside what you (think you) know and considering a problem as if you know nothing at all. But putting aside hard-earned expertise turns out to be quite difficult for many of us. For one thing, it requires admitting you don't know everything, and many people feel their success at work depends on giving the impression that they *do* know things.

To help yourself and your team get there, be clear that you're not asking anyone to ignore their experience or expertise, just to set it aside temporarily so you can see what possibilities that might uncover. It may help to explicitly acknowledge people's expertise and credentials—maybe even make them visible—to mitigate the urge toward impression management that might get in the way of adopting a beginner's mindset. Agree to adopt an approach of being *smart people asking dumb questions on purpose*.

Question Orthodoxies

At the organizational level, creative thinking can be limited by orthodoxies, which are pervasive beliefs that often go unstated and unchallenged. Many times they are not even recognized as beliefs, but more as *what is known to be true*. Orthodoxies can shape strategy and create blind spots. And they can get in the way of breakthrough opportunities because they prevent us from even considering more unconventional solutions.

Some of the more famous orthodoxies that have been toppled in the last few decades relate to the shopping behaviors of consumers. Once upon a time, companies selling shoes and eye glasses were sure people would never buy these items online—that shoppers needed to visit a store to try them on. But new players in the market challenged those orthodoxies and found they weren't facts, but beliefs. And those beliefs were wrong.

Organizational orthodoxies can take many different forms. They could be beliefs about what customers want or don't want, or what they're willing to pay for. They may be assumptions about who your competitors are or what it takes to compete in the market. They might appear as standards for how your organization creates teams, promotes people, or measures performance. Or they could be assumptions about what resources will be available or how those resources will limit your possible actions. *Stripping away everything* requires slowing down and even moving backwards in order to question things you already "know," which makes it a great opportunity to practice some of that healthy skepticism we discuss in the *silence your cynic* chapter and also makes it a powerful complement to our recommendation to *live with the problem*, which we'll discuss in the next chapter.

Although it's all well and good to suggest challenging orthodoxies, it's not always so easy to do. Let's imagine your new team has a big problem to solve. Your team is brainstorming what can be done, and the most senior leader in the room kicks the session off by making a list of *what is known*. Several things make it onto the list that you're wondering about, but no one questions this list—they just nod in agreement and barrel ahead, adding more items and then quickly moving toward brainstorming solutions that are in line with what's on the list. You, however, are wondering, *is* all of that known?

You may be in a position to challenge some orthodoxies, but you're new to the team and the leader is the one who started the list. You may worry that questioning them will make you look clueless. Or you might be concerned about political ramifications—will challenging them make them angry? Maybe you have what you think is a pretty creative solution to the problem, but it doesn't fit with the *what is known* list. Your leader seems very confident about the list and so does everyone else. They've all been around for a long time. You decide your idea is probably not viable and you don't mention it. What a shame.

To help yourself and your team challenge orthodoxies there are several things you can do. For one thing, position *stripping away everything*, not as a denial of science, facts, or knowledge, but as an effort to interrogate beliefs to understand where they come from. Leaders can set the tone and create a space safe for asking questions and challenging assumptions by doing both themselves. Similar to how saying "I'm going to play devil's advocate . . ." can make it easier for some people to challenge what's being said, encourage the use of other phrases that might make people more comfortable: "In the interest of finding the very best solution, let's challenge that assumption." Or, "If I adopt a beginner's mindset, it makes me wonder . . ." And because it can be difficult for people to problem-solve in the abstract, replace the perspective you're asking people to strip away with an alternative. Instead of "Imagine nothing you believe is true," try "Imagine [this alternative] were true."

Don't Believe Everything You Hear

Have you ever heard of the Yerkes-Dodson law? Even if you aren't familiar with its name, you may be familiar with the concept and the visual associated with it—an upside-down *U*-curve illustrating the relationship between stress and performance. This curve suggests that performance suffers in the absence of stress, presumably because there's not enough motivation to perform. Performance then improves with increasing levels of stress, but only up to a point. When stress gets too high, performance starts to decrease again. Sounds reasonable, right? Lots of people think so. Indeed, this "law" is widely referred to and cited in the psychological and managerial literatures, and in the media, too.

You may be interested to know, however, that the Yerkes-Dodson law is based on a study conducted more than 100 years ago with Japanese dancing mice. The mice were exposed to an electric shock and then challenged to learn the difference between a black box and a white box. As it turns out, if you shock a mouse too severely, they don't learn as well. What's particularly interesting is that a study examining the effects of arousal on habit formation in mice was gradually transformed into a managerial law governing the performance of humans in the workplace, and without much evidence to support that leap.

We recently read an interesting analysis, written by Professor Martin Corbett, of how this transformation occurred despite the fact that few published studies have ever replicated the original findings or supported the resulting model.[27] Indeed, Corbett cites a literature review of 52 studies between 1975 and 2000 that found only 4% of them supported the theory that the relationship between stress and performance is shaped like an inverted *U*, and 46% of the studies supported the theory that the relationship is linear and negative. In other words, as stress goes up, performance goes down.[28]

As it turns out, this "law" may not be an accurate representation of how stress affects human performance in the workplace, and yet it's been widely accepted as the truth, and as a result it could guide how many managers and organizations approach employee stress and well-being. And the Yerkes-Dodson law is likely one of many beliefs that may be less than fully supported but that still guides important decisions. Social media has sped up the rate at which information gets shared today, and it has simultaneously made sharing much easier and identifying the source of information much more difficult. That can mean all kinds of claims quickly become common knowledge with very few people having any idea where the "knowledge" came from.

Stripping away everything doesn't mean just dismissing every claim you hear, but instead interrogating it. How do you know this is true? Who said so? Based on what evidence?

Looking for practical ways to boost your breakthrough thinking by *stripping away everything*? Jump ahead to our *strip away everything* methods. We'll guide you through the steps to flip orthodoxies, defy constraints, sleuth for truth, search for UFOs (unidentified fact options), and reuse and repurpose.

Bottom Line Benefits

Strip Away Everything

- Prevents building on a shaky foundation—questioning beliefs and orthodoxies can uncover inaccuracies that might lead to problems later

- Removes limitations—looking past constraints can enable discovery of new directions

- Uncovers new possibilities—challenging an assumption can lead in a fruitful direction, regardless of whether the original assumption ultimately turns out to be true

- Gets more voices into the mix—embracing a beginner's mindset means people don't need to be experts to contribute in valuable ways

- Increases awareness—sometimes you don't even realize what's holding you back until you start looking

Breakthrough
YOU

Strip Away Everything

Team problem-solving isn't the only place where your beliefs can limit you. Your life is affected daily by what you believe, sometimes in ways that aren't even apparent to you. The decisions you make, the actions you take, and the ways you experience situations and life events are all shaped by underlying beliefs.

If there is an area of your life that feels particularly challenging, stressful, or unsatisfying for you, it may be fruitful to work on uncovering the beliefs underlying those circumstances. Then, explore the impact of questioning those beliefs. We're not talking about *stripping away* your core values about what's important in life, rather surfacing the perspective from which you're viewing things and questioning whether there is another perspective that might shift your experience, actions, and decisions about how to live your life.

For example, maybe someone (let's name that someone Taylor) is working a lot of hours in hopes of getting a promotion. Perhaps Taylor is still managing to carve out time for family but has had to forgo time with friends and involvement in community events. Taylor may not love working quite so much but believes that's what it takes to move up, and maybe if successful, Taylor expects to have more responsibility and a bigger paycheck, but also possibly even less free time.

What do these actions suggest about Taylor's beliefs? Is advancement more important than time with friends? Are more responsibility and a bigger paycheck more valuable than community involvement? Viewing actions as evidence suggests the answer both of these questions, for Taylor, is yes.

If Taylor really doesn't like working quite so much, what might the benefit be of challenging those underlying beliefs? What if friends were more important than advancement—how would that influence Taylor's choices? Suppose being involved in the community was more valuable than increasing responsibility and salary—what would that mean for Taylor's future path? There isn't a universal right answer to any of these questions. The power is in asking them and understanding your own answers, and then exploring what that means for how you'll live your life.

There are many other underlying beliefs that shape your life. Does the way in which you're living your life suggest you hold any of the beliefs that follow? How would it affect your life to challenge those beliefs?

- I should always be aiming for a promotion to the next step on the ladder.

- I need to respond to this email right away.

- I should be able to handle whatever is happening because someone else was able to.

- I'll be a success once I achieve *x, y,* or *z.*

- If I'm not out of my comfort zone, I'm not growing.

- Logic is superior to emotion.

- My worth is determined by the size of my paycheck.

Avoid rushing to the solution.
Better things come to those who explore before acting.

Copyright © 2023 Deloitte Development LLC. All rights reserved.

If you've ever been called out for "admiring the problem" we'll bet it was more of an accusation than a commendation. Once a problem has been identified, there is often an assumption that it should be solved, and preferably as soon as possible. Contemplation without action tends to be viewed as unproductive. But what if taking a bit more time to explore the problem could help you solve it more efficiently? What if it could reveal new dimensions, perspectives, and opportunities?

Imagine you manage a large data-entry team, and in reviewing your latest monthly report, you notice a spike in the overall error rate, a key performance metric. You immediately request that your team leads speak to their people about being more careful, sure that will solve the problem. But next month's report tells you it didn't help, so you decide to put some incentives in place to encourage precision. Another month later the teams still haven't improved. Now you're getting annoyed and switch from carrot to stick—writing up those who make errors. Although lots of people get written up, the error rate doesn't budge. You escalate to letting people go and are hopeful that will finally fix it, but three *more* months later, it hasn't made a bit of difference.

Then one day, as you're puzzling over the problem, you overhear your teenager saying how *boring* school is. You wonder if your team might be bored, so you shuffle them around and relocate each individual to a new work station. A month later, your report reveals something peculiar. Although the error rate hasn't changed, different people are making mistakes. You realize the errors are associated with certain work stations, not individual people, and digging a bit further reveals the keyboards were replaced in all the high error stations around when the errors started. A quick online search tells you that those keyboards have since been recalled. Problem solved—finally!

Although we'd like to congratulate you on getting to the bottom of things, we can't help but think of the six months it took to do so, not to mention the people who lost their jobs because you were essentially solving for the wrong problem. In your rush to fix the issue, it seems you made an assumption that led you to solve for careless employees instead of faulty keyboards. If it's any comfort, you're far from alone. It's all too common to jump into problem-solving mode before making an effort to deeply understand the problem itself—to make assumptions and fail to examine them, as we discuss in the *strip away everything* chapter.

The remedy? When you're up against a big challenge, *live with the problem* awhile. Invest time in understanding a problem deeply before attempting to solve it. Get curious and explore it. We're not suggesting you avoid the problem or passively accept something that needs to be fixed. We just mean to take a beat before you charge in to develop solutions. But how do you really live with a problem in a way that's not just a waste of time? By looking before you leap, trying passive percolation, and spending your time wisely.

Stories from the Field

Live with the Problem

A leadership team came to us for help reducing their high rate of employee turnover. The team felt strongly that the root of the problem was dissatisfaction with compensation, and that was the planned focus for our work with them. But instead of jumping right into solving for the compensation problem, we took a step back to get curious about the turnover they were experiencing in their organization. We shared internal and external data, featured employee testimonials, and highlighted feedback gathered from individuals who had left the company—not only in their moment of exit but months later when they'd moved on to other jobs.

As we explored this information, the team developed a new perspective on the core problem. They came to understand that compensation was only part of the story. Employees were also dissatisfied with the opportunities available for growth. And in fact, they were even willing to trade some level of compensation in return for more career pathways, better mentorship, and commitment to development. This new clarity on the multifaceted and interrelated cause of the turnover led the group on a path to a whole different set of solutions than a compensation solution alone would have.

Look Before You Leap

Often people are quite confident they already know what problem they're solving for, but as in our keyboard example, it may not always be what you first think it is. It seemed at first that the problem was a spike in errors, but that was really a symptom of another problem, and the errors couldn't be solved for until the root cause was understood. That, too, was easily mistaken at first, as it seemed the employees were likely to blame. And that wasn't irrational—if employees are making errors, it's reasonable to assume they're not being careful enough. If one abides by the principle of Occam's razor—that the simplest explanation is often the best—it would be quite justifiable to blame the employees. But a more precise application of Occam's razor specifies the best explanation is the simplest one that *is consistent with available data*. If you move too quickly, you may not even realize that there's data you might have considered. (Like the data showing particular keyboards were making errors, not particular employees.)

To have the best chance of reaching breakthrough, take time to observe what's actually happening and gather more data before you start on solving. How do you know what the problem really is? What data exist or could be gathered? What input might other people have? Do key stakeholders agree on what you're trying to solve for?

In our example, it was eventually discovered that the keyboards were faulty. And that, quite obviously, required a very different solution than either careless or bored employees would have. Take the time to understand what you're actually solving for and ensure it's the root problem rather than just a symptom of the problem.

One clear benefit of spending more time on the problem up front is that it can help you avoid wasted time, effort, and resources later on. Getting clear on the right problem can reduce the need for rework, moving backwards, or worse yet, sticking with the wrong path because you've already invested so much. Humans tend to be vulnerable to the sunk cost fallacy, whereby one sticks with a direction, even when it clearly doesn't make sense anymore, because so much has been invested already.[29] Sometimes those investments are in the form of money, but other times they are in the form of effort, time, emotions, or reputational currency. In our keyboard example, you might have been tempted to continue focusing on the employees so that you didn't have to admit to firing people for something that was not their fault, a far from ideal situation. The best way to deal with an issue like that? Avoid it in the first place by getting more clarity on the problem before rushing to solve it.

Try Passive Percolation

Sometimes solving a problem quickly is seen as the most critical measure of success, even if that means an inferior solution. We'll bet you've felt this pressure to elevate speed above all else, whether from your leadership, the market, or other stakeholders. As the pace of change in the world accelerates, the ability to move quickly is not an advantage, but a minimum entry requirement.

Or maybe you're not feeling much outside pressure, but still feel an internal pressure to get things done. One study we conducted with more than 13,000 professionals identified a feeling of accomplishment as the top career priority.[30] And what better accomplishment is there than solving a really tough problem? Moreover, this desire to act quickly may be even stronger in stressful situations. In another study we conducted with more than 17,000 professionals, we found that the most common strategy for coping with stress is jumping in and taking action.[31]

We certainly understand those external and internal pressures—we feel them, too. But here's the thing: understanding the problem more deeply before acting on it can eventually enable solving it more swiftly, and more effectively. In our keyboard example, slowing down to explore the problem more deeply might have led to making the connection to new keyboards months earlier than when the problem was assumed to be caused by careless employees and there was a rush to address that.

But *living with the problem* awhile can help you reach breakthrough even if you don't spend the time actively trying to understand the problem. Maybe you know what it's like to have a hard time writing something. We do! Sometimes the words just don't flow, and it can feel like an impossible chore to get them down. You stare at the screen and wrestle with your thoughts, you try to spit the words out but struggle to express what you want to say, you scroll on your phone and put it off a little longer. And then you realize the day has gone and you haven't gotten your writing done, so you close your laptop feeling frustrated. The next day you get back to it and the words roll off your fingertips as if coming from somewhere else, and you can't figure out why it was so difficult the day before.

Sometimes when you can't solve something, whether that's how to get the right words down or some other challenge, it's enough just to let some time pass. And although passing time sounds passive, there is plenty of activity going on in your brain as the minutes and hours roll by. When you sleep, for example, your brain is organizing things, but also when you daydream, walk, do the dishes, or whatever.[32] When you're not actively thinking about something, your brain is still there tossing ideas about undercover. And sometimes when you come back to the problem later—ta da! The answer is clear.

We've seen this effect very clearly in the Deloitte Greenhouse. Prior to COVID-19, we almost always delivered experiences in person and in a single day. When the world went virtual, we found that eight or nine hours on Zoom was entirely too many, so now we typically deliver virtual experiences over two or more days with shorter sessions. And we've seen that participants often come back on the second day with fresh ideas or a different perspective that they didn't leave with at the end of the first day. That time in between—to do other things while ideas rattle around in their brains, to talk with someone else, or to sleep on it—can really make a difference.

Barriers to Breakthrough

77% of the people we surveyed indicated they might hesitate to contribute if they haven't had time to think through or prepare for a discussion in advance.

When you encourage your team to **live with the problem** awhile, it can enable more opportunities for those who like to consider and reflect before they speak.

There's another reason to take your time when you need a truly breakthrough solution: although many people believe that they're more creative under time pressure, research suggests they're actually less so. A study in which 7,000 professionals kept journals of their activities and also rated their sense of time pressure found that more time pressure on a certain day meant less creative thinking for the next *three* days.[33] Not exactly a recipe for breakthrough. In a similar vein, a review of more than 100 studies suggests you may be most creative when you spend a bit of time wrestling with a problem, then take a break, then come back to it later.[34] Living with the problem awhile can give you more time to do that.

Spend Your Time Wisely

One great thing about living with the problem is that it gives you more space to integrate the other principles we're recommending. Remember the hidden and not so hidden assumptions we discuss in the *strip away everything* chapter? Living with the problem gives you time to explore, question, and challenge those assumptions before you jump to solving. One of the best ways to take advantage of your additional time is to ask *why*, repeatedly.

In our *story from the field* for this chapter, we share an example of a team solving for high rates of turnover. To do so, they needed more clarity on the root of the problem. *Why* were people leaving? The team was pretty clear on that—people were leaving because they were dissatisfied. So it wasn't actually turnover they needed to solve for, but dissatisfaction. But *why* were people dissatisfied? Initially the team thought it was because of compensation, but they ultimately learned that a lack of opportunities for growth was also contributing.

Asking *why* enabled the team to progress from the problem of high turnover to the problem of dissatisfaction with compensation and opportunities for growth. That was certainly helpful but didn't provide enough clarity to really solve the problem because they could still have been making some faulty assumptions. They needed to get even closer to the root by asking *why* yet again. *Why* are people dissatisfied with their compensation? Because they're actually underpaid compared to the market? Because they don't have enough information to make that judgment? Because they perceive inequity among employees? Or something else?

Why are people dissatisfied with opportunities for growth? Because they feel it takes too long to reach the next rung on the ladder? Because they don't understand what's expected of them in order to be offered those opportunities? Because they want more varied options for how to grow? Or something else?

The best solutions for any one of these possibilities would likely be different than the best solutions for the others. And each time you ask *why*, you get underneath more assumptions and get a bit closer to the root of the problem—to what you really need to be solving for.

In the upcoming chapters we'll discuss many other ways in which you can use your time wisely while *living with the problem* awhile. In the chapter on *enlisting a motley crew* we'll discuss the benefits of bringing together diverse perspectives. Doing so isn't always easy and working across differences can take time. When you commit to *living with the problem* awhile, you give yourself time to do that important work instead of glossing over it. It can also leave more space for getting to know each other as humans—the importance of which we'll discuss in the *get real* chapter—and for very human processes like emotions to enter into your work. Research has suggested that strong emotions can be detrimental to creativity, but milder emotions can enhance it.[35] Slowing down can allow time for emotions to build, crest, and dissipate before you get to the solving stage. We'll also soon discuss the importance of honesty in the chapter on *not playing "nice."* Although honesty can help you move things along quickly, it can also cause delays if you don't take the time to deliver candid messages with care. When you ease off time pressure you allow space for very important discussions to occur.

Looking for practical ways to boost your breakthrough thinking by *living with the problem*? Jump ahead to our *live with the problem* methods. We'll guide you through the steps to act like a toddler, change the lens, try question storming, stretch out your brainstorming, and sleep on it.

Bottom Line Benefits

Live with the Problem

- Gives space to understand what problem you should really be solving—it's not always what you first think it is

- Avoids wasted time, effort, and resources by helping ensure you're solving for the root cause and not just the symptoms

- Offers your subconscious an incubation period to mull the problem over for a while, which increases insight and creativity

- Provides an opportunity to gather input and different perspectives. Do key stakeholders agree on what you're trying to solve for?

- Allows time for emotions to build, crest, and dissipate

Breakthrough YOU

Live with the Problem

If you're anything like us, you're currently living with many real-life problems. Maybe one of those problems is constant cravings for sweet or savory snacks. (But we're just guessing.) When faced with such cravings, there are basically two options: to eat or not to eat. And if you are happy with choosing *to eat*, then go for it and skip to the next section. But if you'd prefer to choose *not to eat*, you might be able to master living with the problem—with the craving—long enough for it to dissipate.

Evan Forman, professor and director of the Drexel University Center for Weight, Eating, and Lifestyle Science shared with the *New York Times* that "You don't have to make cravings go away, but you also don't have to eat because of them."[36] *We don't?* This was a bit of a headscratcher for us when we first read it. It certainly *feels* like we have to eat when we have a craving. But by reading more of what he had to say, we came to understand that Forman was talking about a mindful approach to living with the problem of a craving. The technique of *urge surfing* is based on the idea that an urge or craving is like a wave. If you're in the ocean, waves are natural and inevitable. You can't stop them and fighting them won't work either. An individual wave can be a strong force, but it doesn't really last that long. You can ride it out as it builds, crests, and then dissipates. Likewise, cravings are natural and inevitable. If you ride it out, even a strong craving typically builds, crests, and dissipates.

Here are the steps to riding the wave of a craving:

1. Notice and acknowledge the craving. Think or say, "I'm having a craving for chocolate." (Or whatever you're craving.)

2. Remind yourself that the craving isn't likely to last very long.

3. Observe the craving—get curious about it. Where do you feel it? What does it feel like?

4. Accept the craving. Don't try to suppress it, fight it, or distract yourself from it.

5. Wait awhile, paying attention and staying open to what happens next.

6. Congratulate yourself on your "surfing" aptitude.

What's *Business Chemistry*® got to do with this?

In 2018 we shared with the world Deloitte's approach to working style differences in our book *Business Chemistry: Practical Magic for Crafting Powerful Work Relationships*.[37] We highlighted four primary working styles. As it turns out, these different styles are often relevant for how people approach problem-solving and solution generation, and thus they play a role in developing and enhancing one's breakthrough thinking prowess. We'll explore these differences further relative to the principles, but for now we offer a quick refresher on the four types themselves:

PIONEERS value possibilities and they spark energy and imagination. They're outgoing, spontaneous, and adaptable. They're creative thinkers who believe big risks can bring great things.

GUARDIANS value stability and they bring order and rigor. They're practical, detail-oriented, and reserved. They're deliberate decision-makers apt to stick with the status quo.

DRIVERS value challenge and they generate momentum. They're technical, quantitative, and logical. They're direct in their approach to people and problems.

INTEGRATORS value connection and they draw teams together. They're empathic, diplomatic, and relationship oriented. They're attuned to nuance, seeing shades of gray rather than black and white.

CHECK YOUR EDGE

Ask yourself, "Is this truly unexpected?" Surprise is the mother of inspiration.

Copyright © 2023 Deloitte Development LLC. All rights reserved.

CHAPTER

04

One of the most common human phobias is the fear of heights.[38] Standing on the edge of a sheer drop—even watching someone else stand on an edge—can cause visceral discomfort. A precipice is a *literal* transition point between security and risk, between known and uncertain, between stasis and movement. And although you may rarely find yourself on an actual cliff's edge, a similar edge exists *metaphorically* when you're poised between the status quo and change. Though that edge may not seem as scary as an actual abyss, you might be equally reluctant to toe it.

We've already mentioned the status quo bias—human beings have a preference for the ways things currently are—a predilection popularized by Daniel Kahneman, Jack Knetsch, and Richard Thaler in their work on behavioral economics.[39] This desire may be rational, keeping you in a secure space, but it can also be irrational, causing you to stay in a rut that may be contrary to your best interests or that may not push you to your full potential. And certainly, when it comes to breakthrough thinking, such inertia can be problematic. There's a reason for the old adage, "Nothing ventured, nothing gained."

Consider the company Fujifilm, for instance, who was seeing growth and profitability in the physical film space even as digital photography began to take off. Their status quo commitment to physical film was a success—they even became a market leader. But rather than trying to stay in their safety zone of the photography market, the company pivoted to leverage their technology and research in other industries, specifically pharmaceuticals, health care, and even cosmetics. This self-disruption enabled Fujifilm to not only survive but thrive as the digital photography trend matured.[40]

However, change just for change's sake does not a breakthrough make. The infamous failure of "New Coke" provides a great case in point. Mistakenly believing that the Coca-Cola flavor needed to be modified to compete, Coke executives decided to roll out a new formula touted as "smoother, rounder, yet bolder—a more harmonious flavor." Far from being the market booster they were looking for, this change offended loyal Coke drinkers and created enormous consumer backlash. Ultimately the company backpedaled and reintroduced the original, "classic," version.[41]

The principle of *checking your edge* is about finding a healthy balance. It's about pushing your thinking and asking whether your ideas are truly innovative or unique. It's about recognizing the tendency to stick to the status quo, whereas breakthrough thinking requires actively seeking your metaphorical edges to help spark innovation. Once you've discovered those edges, you're not obligated to hurl yourself willy-nilly beyond them, but rather to use them as provocation for fresh thinking and new growth. To consciously decide whether, and how, to take that next leap.

The difficult thing about edges though, particularly metaphorical ones, is that you're not always aware of them. Picture, if you will, a circle with you at its center. This circle is the comfort zone. You, your team, and your organization all have comfort zones. Things may not necessarily be perfect in this circle, but they are familiar and understood by you, and you are relatively capable, in

Stories from the Field

Check Your Edge

Several years ago, we started doing a different kind of experience with senior executives. In the middle of a session, a man would walk into the room holding a guitar. This man, friend and co-conspirator Cliff Goldmacher, would introduce himself as a song writer and inform this group of business leaders that they themselves would now compose and perform their own songs.

When we first piloted this experience (*checking our own edge*), we were confident that people would engage with the songwriting piece—after all, that's a relatively intellectual exercise—but we were a bit concerned they might resist the performance part. We were wrong. In session after session we saw universal participation, with teams enthusiastically bellowing out their songs in front of their assembled peers.

In speaking with executives following these events, we heard a recurring theme captured well in the words of one CEO, "We do difficult presentations all the time, speaking to shareholders, interacting with the board, talking to the press. But that's our job and we're used to it. This made me uncomfortable in a good way. I feel like my brain is firing in new ways—it's exhilarating."

Asking executives to stretch themselves a bit outside of their comfort zone in an unexpected way helped them get to "flow state," activating their intelligence in a fresh way and led to much richer and more provocative subsequent discussion and insights.

control, and anxiety free within the boundaries. You can, and do, accomplish a lot in this comfort zone. It's your performance home base, of sorts. But to stay at the center of this circle, as comfortable as it may be, limits breakthrough potential. Edges, by definition, sit at the periphery, and you won't find them unless you expand your thinking, pursue the unexpected, and stretch yourself beyond where you may feel comfortable.

Expand Your Thinking

Imagine yourself happily ensconced in a valley surrounded by mountains. You have lived in this valley for a long time, and you know the landscape in your field of vision very well. Your daily view is of the valley floor itself and the peaks all around you, but you can't really see anything beyond those ranges.

Now imagine that one day you hike to the edge of that valley and climb one of those peaks and look around. How does your view change? Perhaps you see more mountains? Perhaps you see something different, like an ocean or a town?

By venturing to this new vantage point, you've changed your field of vision. The act of actively moving beyond your ordinary way of looking at things (the valley) to the unfamiliar (the top of the mountain peak) gets you to an edge.

The hike to get there likely took effort. It might have even felt (or in fact been) dangerous, heading beyond the known geography of the valley. But as a result, you can see a broader vista.

You may still choose to go back to the valley after seeing that view, or you may choose to continue on through the mountain range. The intent of *checking your edge* is not to necessarily step beyond it. Rather, it's to gain access to a whole new set of information, options, and opportunities.

In the real world, you can find this edge by recognizing what "valley" you find yourself in. Are you always working in the same spaces, meeting with the same customers, talking about the same topics? What are the norms that make up your landscape? Is your team or organization hierarchical, tradition bound, insular? What are the well-worn paths of process that you tend to tread? Do you follow rote and rules, deflect decisions, dodge conflict? What are the major features on which you anchor your explorations? Is there a central philosophy, standard framework, cultural belief? By creating this mental map of the status quo, you're able to start testing its frontiers. You can ask yourselves key questions such as these:

- Is this thing I'm thinking about truly innovative, or is it already on the map—perhaps just called by a different name?

- How could I get a different perspective on this or find a better vantage point?

- Are there other explorers who might be able to enhance, or expand on, my current view?

The Power of Partnering Up

When you're trying to see things from a new vantage point, divergent thinking can help. Divergent thinking is the process of coming up with many different possible ideas that spread out in a multitude of directions. Convergent thinking, by contrast, is about narrowing down to a select few. Both are important in the creative process, but if you don't diverge first, you are literally limiting your view of the potential idea set and thus decreasing the probability of breakthrough thinking.

Some people (like our *Business Chemistry* Pioneers) revel in this type of divergent creative process. They embrace imaginative, novel possibilities and are much more comfortable with ambiguity than others. They are the ones eager to hike out of the valley to explore the peak, or perhaps even to suggest a whole new way of getting there (Hot air balloons! Trained condors!).

But this breakthrough principle isn't just about getting to the edge, it's about checking it. And checking implies analysis, evaluation, and thoughtful consideration. This is a strength more strongly expressed by other styles (including the Pioneer's opposite, the Guardian) and brings the balancing convergence to the divergent exploration.

Although some rare individuals may possess the ability to combine both divergent and convergent thinking, for most people it helps to partner up.[42] Combining different thinking styles and applying them strategically helps to see that new vantage point (divergence) but also be thoughtful about what to do next (convergence).

Asking these questions requires incremental effort to go beyond the usual routine and depart from the comfort of the center. But, in turn, it could yield richer, and perhaps unexpected, new insights.

Pursue the Unexpected

A more expansive view is only one of the benefits to be found at the edge. An additional boon is the potential for surprise. Although humans tend to be biased toward the status quo, and indeed often spend significant effort planning and preparing to avoid surprises, there is also great benefit, even pleasure, to be gained from the unforeseen.[43]

Unexpected situations spark your brain, heightening your senses and emotions. This applies for positive surprises as well as negative ones. When you're surprised, you're jolted out of the analgesia of the day to day and forced to focus on the novelty that has entered your life. Your creativity is amplified, as is your memory and ability to learn.[44]

Checking your edge is about not only going beyond the familiar, but intentionally seeking the surprising. Sometimes surprises occur naturally; by venturing out far enough, you will experience novel things that can stimulate your mind. But other times, you need to engineer surprises for yourself.

One of our favorite props in our Deloitte Greenhouse spaces is the backward bike. Initially a prank developed by the friends of YouTuber/engineer Destin Sandlin, the bike has an unusual design modification: if you turn the handlebars to the right the front tire goes to the left, and vice versa.[45] Although this seems like a simple enough change, the effect is striking. It is unexpectedly hard to ride this bike, as you essentially need to retrain your brain. By creating this visceral surprise experience, we push people out of their comfort zones and jolt their brains.

Surprises don't need to be actual physical things and experiences, though. Think back for a moment to our example of that comfortable valley and your hike to see beyond your familiar field of vision. As we described, after hiking to the edge, your new view will look different, and seeing an ocean or a town beyond your familiar peaks may be unanticipated and could provide that injection of novelty we need to spark breakthrough thinking.

But what if you got to that new edge and found yourself surrounded by fog, unable to make out anything? What if, in that situation, you set your imagination free and envisaged what could be beyond that mist? Perhaps alien skies teeming with spaceships. Or a country made of candy with licorice roads and sugar spun trees. Or an Orwell-inspired cityscape with farm animals driving cars, sitting in cafes, and talking on mobile phones. That would be quite astonishing.

It doesn't matter that these examples are far-fetched. Indeed, that's the point. This degree of departure from what the mind expects is precisely what makes it powerful for breakthrough thinking. Brainstorming what *might* be beyond the edge can be as effective as actually seeing beyond the edge. Research by professor Justin Berg has shown that spending a short time (as little as six minutes) attempting to develop original ideas led people to be more open to novelty and better able to recognize the potential in other people's ideas.[46]

You can be an agent in seeding your own breakthrough thinking by imagining surprising possibilities at the edge. For instance, picture a meeting in which someone has drawn a life-size door on the wall, labeled "The Future," slightly ajar and complete with a doorknob looking ready to be fully opened. What kind of discussion might ensue about what's on the other side of that door? How might that discussion potentially differ from simply asking a question such as, "What do you think are the key characteristics of the future?" Both approaches will likely provide interesting insights and perspectives, but the former approach is far more likely than the latter to reveal unusual threads and possibilities.

You can also increase your chances of experiencing the unpredictable by challenging yourself to break routine, defy habit, or forge a different trail. Strip a meeting room of the traditional boardroom table and replace it with bean bags. Host a discussion in a park with a picnic lunch themed to the topic. Take a field trip to literally walk in the shoes of your customers or stakeholders. Try to seek, like Robert Frost, the path less traveled by. That could make all the difference.

Stretch Yourself

Breakthrough thinking thrives when you check edges, not only around the context in which you see and evaluate the world, but also around how you draw the boundaries of your own capabilities and potential. People often underestimate themselves. They assume their comfort zone "abyss" is closer than it actually is because they've never tried to find their personal edges.

Venturing out from the core of your individual comfort zone can be stressful, but it can help to think of this zone not as an absolute—you're either in it or you're not—but rather as a gradient. The center is where you're most established and secure. As you move outward, you can see that there isn't a rigid boundary or drop off, but rather an organic edge that continues to change and expand over time as you grow your skills and extend your experiences.

The intent with stretching is not to force yourself completely outside of your circle—that could feel terrifying. Instead, the objective is to go far enough that you can thoughtfully grow that edge and expand the scope of your comfort zone. Like a scene from the *Indiana Jones and the Last Crusade* movie, this might take a little faith that you're not in fact stepping into an abyss, but rather discovering an extension of your edge.

One way to do this is by trying to find your flow state. Flow state is when you are fully engaged, involved, and enjoying an activity to the point where the world around you almost disappears.[47] This is sometimes called being "in the zone." This zone is not the same as your comfort zone, though it builds on it. Flow requires a beyond-average challenge, something perhaps a little bit scary or intimidating—*not* your familiar, everyday tasks, but also not petrifying.

What turns that challenge into productive performance though, versus potentially paralyzing anxiety, is a correspondingly high level of skill. This skill is the part that is familiar to you and that comes from your comfort zone. The challenge is the way you're applying that skill to push your edge. When you're seeking flow state, you're not hurtling your body down your first black diamond ski trail never having skied before. You're taking a new, difficult run where your capabilities are up to the challenge.

Flow state is associated with altered brain function, including suppressed brain activation in structures linked to thinking about oneself and negative thoughts, and increased activation in reward processing areas.[48] So not only can flow state help you to expand your edge, it feels good, too.

We believe that one of the reasons seeking flow is an effective way to *check your edge* is that giving yourself a challenge just beyond what you're comfortable doing stretches you without breaking you. It provides an opportunity to surprise yourself with what you're capable of and lets you develop new muscles to grow that edge. Your ability to apply these novel skills in turn gives you the other definition of edge—a powerful advantage when it comes to breakthrough.

Looking for practical ways to boost your breakthrough thinking by *checking your edge*? Jump ahead to our *check your edge* methods. We'll guide you through the steps to plot your portfolio, think three bears, play Mad Libs, mix it up, and push yourself.

Bottom Line Benefits

Check Your Edge

- Pushes you to look beyond the comfort of the status quo, revealing new vantage points and opportunities

- Provides fuel for fresh thinking

- Sparks creativity and imagination by introducing surprise and novelty

- Unlocks individual potential by stretching personal capabilities

- Increases the likelihood of flow state and associated performance improvements

Breakthrough YOU

Check Your Edge

Perhaps you're one of the 70% or so of people who have a fear of public speaking.[49] You believe beyond a shadow of a doubt that the second you step onto a stage with an audience full of people, your tongue will dry out and latch itself to the top of your mouth, your brain will empty of every carefully practiced word you were planning to say, and your heart will start racing to the point where either you'll pass out, the audience will hear it, or both.

You could just avoid all public speaking, or you could check your edge by just shifting a little bit away from your comfort zone. For instance, what if you didn't start with the TED Talk forum? What if instead you decided to speak up and say something at a large-group meeting? Or make a toast at a dinner party? Or introduce a speaker (using note cards if you like!) at a small event? Yes, you may still have palpitations, but chances are it will go better than you feared. You will be stepping outward from your comfort zone while proving to yourself that that journey is survivable.

Why bother? Because if you don't *check your edge*, you might assume you are bounded by an insurmountable wall between possible and not possible. You may keep yourself from trying things that could actually bring you great personal satisfaction and success.

So think of that thing you've been avoiding, that edge that seems scary and extreme, and ask yourself, "How can I move closer to this edge without going over it?" And then as much as possible, buckle your seatbelt, shift into drive, and enjoy the ride.

––––––––––––

ENLIST A MOTLEY CREW

Go beyond the usual suspects.

Sparks fly when thinkers, domains,
and outside disciplines collide.

Copyright © 2023 Deloitte Development LLC. All rights reserved.

You likely know what it's like to be stuck in an airport waiting for a delayed plane. Sometimes good company makes this frustrating situation a little more palatable, and other times your airport company is a bit less enjoyable. Maybe you can relate to both scenarios. But have you ever selected someone for your team because you thought you could enjoy being stuck in an airport with them? This is an actual screening technique, commonly known as the *airport test*. It can create teams who bond easily and have a really great time together, but there's a problem. People often prefer others who think a lot like them—this is called the *similarity bias*.[50] And it might be okay to limit your company to those that think like you if you're just waiting for a delayed plane or maybe having a drink in the airport bar, but if your team has some really challenging problems to solve, homogeneity is unlikely to do you a lot of favors. Indeed, just the opposite may be what you need.

We're not suggesting there aren't any benefits at all to working with people who have a similar perspective. It can be very comforting and even productive. If you're a creative type, being around other creatives can inspire you to new heights of innovation. If you're a detail person, it can be a relief to work with others who get the importance of the little things. But these feel-good scenarios can also lead to some undesirable outcomes. Too many creative types together can waste a lot of time and money chasing one impractical idea after another and then abandoning each before bringing them to fruition. If you all see yourselves as the idea people, who is focused on execution? Likewise, too many detailed people can get trapped in a state of analysis paralysis, make very little progress, and end up choking on the dust of their competitors. If you're all focused on the minutiae, who's keeping an eye on the horizon and making sure you move forward in a timely way?

Instead of looking for others who think a lot like you, you'll likely gain more from including people who think quite differently. That team of creative, big-picture thinkers could probably benefit from a few teammates with a penchant for thinking through the specifics of implementation. And that detail-obsessed team could probably use someone encouraging them to make their way out of the weeds.

When you include someone who thinks differently, they may see things you don't or see them from a different angle. They may consider problems and potential solutions in ways that can shift your perspective. Diversity of thought means more perspectives on a problem and also more potential solutions to consider. It can lead teams to examine issues more thoroughly, articulate thoughts more clearly, and challenge and test assumptions. Ultimately, it can increase creativity, improve problem-solving and decision-making, and benefit the bottom line.[51]

Frans Johansson wrote in his book *The Medici Effect* that "the most powerful innovation happens at the 'intersection,' where ideas and concepts from diverse industries, cultures, and disciplines collide."[52] To find those intersections, scrap the airport test and instead set your sights on *enlisting a motley crew*. In other words, go beyond the usual suspects and seek varied perspectives on a problem, maybe even from outside your own team or discipline. To understand how you can get to breakthrough, we'll share what it means to get truly motley, to enlist all members, and then to row like a crew.

Stories from the Field

Enlist a Motley Crew

We once hosted a consortium of health care professionals to develop a pathogens strategy with the goal of preventing future pandemics. Some of the individuals had worked together in the past and had experienced much success confronting other outbreaks. However, with the world just over a year into the COVID-19 pandemic, the stakes for such a group felt higher than ever. With this in mind (and benefiting from the COVID-induced ability to gather virtually), we decided to expand the slate of voices in the conversation to get a holistic view of the entire nation's health care system. We had a *motley crew* of participation including nurses, PAs, doctors, hospital administrators, insurance executives, research PhDs, and EMS professionals from all over the country.

Just the act of bringing all these voices together felt important and new, and the combination of fresh faces and diverse voices added energy to the cause. Following the first meeting, the group still had so much left to discuss that they arranged another virtual gathering. Their conversation was even more fruitful the second time because they now had diversity of thought and earned trust in the room. This series of collaborations led to a huge, stepping stone victory when, based on their robust, breakthrough ideas, the group received funding for the continued development of their strategy.

Get Truly Motley

On March 5, 2022, explorer Earnest Shackleton's ill-fated ship, the *Endurance*, was found at the bottom of the Weddell Sea in Antarctica.[53] It had been more than 100 years since the ship was crushed by ice and sunk. We were particularly interested in the discovery because we featured Shackleton as the consummate Pioneer in our book *Business Chemistry*.[54] For this principle, it's his crew that's relevant, all 27 of whom survived the 20-month ordeal of being trapped on the polar ice pack.

The group of men Shackleton selected for that inauspicious voyage were truly a motley crew. Starting with 5,000 applications, the final assemblage included a number of "able seaman"—critical for such an undertaking—but also men with expertise in navigation, meteorology, physics, engineering, carpentry, surgery, biology, cooking, photography, and art.[55] The diversity of skills associated with these official roles likely contributed to their survival, but many of the men adopted unofficial roles that were also indispensable—an expert penguin catcher, a banjo player, and a number of amateur actors who kept the crew entertained through the long cold months.

Consider your own teams at work. Do they possess a similar level of diversity? Do they have a breadth of experiences and perspectives? Of expertise and approaches? Would they be likely to survive such a harrowing ordeal—even the corporate equivalent of it? Are they likely to reach breakthrough?

A group with any diversity at all could be seen as a motley crew, but there are levels of diversity and levels of motley. Let's say you've got a really tough problem to solve, so you gather the top brass in your department—those with the most experience—but you notice they're all women. So maybe you pull in some of the most experienced men, and you give yourself a little pat on the back because you've increased the diversity of your group and also its level of motley. But then maybe you remember what you learned in the *strip away everything* chapter, and you wonder how good this group will be at embracing a beginner's mindset. You consider that it might be a good thing to add a few people who haven't been working on this particular problem quite so long, and you add a few junior team members.

You've now got even more diversity and an even higher level of motley. Even so, you start to think about the fact that everyone works in the same department and, in some sense, might have similar ways of approaching problems. You wonder, could you bring someone in from a different department, or from a totally different industry or discipline, maybe? They truly would have a beginner's mindset in relation to this particular problem. And then it occurs to you that it might be helpful to have more than one outside perspective, so you invite a few more people from other disciplines. When you combine these new folks with the experts you've already got, you really are starting to have a motley crew that's likely to be more creative in its problem-solving.

As our example suggests, to get truly motley, you'll want to consider multiple layers of diversity. The initial impulse to add some men to a team made up exclusively of women was a good one, and it made the team more diverse. But it didn't really start to approach being a motley crew until a few more layers of diversity were added. Breakthrough is facilitated by different ways of thinking, and many layers of diversity are more likely to get you closer than one layer.

A Note About Intersectionality

To keep things simple, we've been talking about lenses and layers of diversity as if they are (1) homogeneous and (2) independent from one another. Yet we acknowledge that in reality they are neither. Women aren't all the same, nor are all accountants. Moreover, no woman is *only* a woman—she also has an ethnicity, a *Business Chemistry* type, a functional expertise, and lots of other identities that together make up who she is and what perspective(s) she'll bring to a team. The same goes for accountants. And diversity is defined by visible and invisible characteristics, like an iceberg with a portion rising above the water and an even larger portion below. Every team has *some* diversity—even one made up of only women or only accountants. But each additional lens on diversity provides an opportunity to explore whether a crew can get just a bit more motley.

Although having multiple layers of diversity on your team is important, so is the balance of different perspectives. Adding just a teammate or two with a different perspective may not get you the effect you're hoping for, because a team with a majority type tends to favor that type's perspective, overshadowing those of any minorities. And research has repeatedly shown that single individuals with a different perspective are often not heard.[56] Just imagine one voice trying to rise above the din of Shackleton's rowdy crew. Two voices are more likely to be heard than just one, but three represents a magic number of sorts when it comes to gaining a group's attention. An individual may be more willing to speak up if there is at least one other who disagrees with the group, but it's the power of the third voice that lets them be heard.

To get a sense of how balanced your team is, consider how ecological diversity is measured, because teams are a bit like ecosystems. Simpson's Diversity Index is one example that takes into account both the *number* of species in a given ecosystem and the *balance* of species.[57] By this measure, having some outside perspectives in a group makes it more diverse than having only insiders, but if the insiders overwhelm the outsiders, the group's diversity index will be lower than if it's more equally distributed. And that could mean your team is less likely to achieve breakthrough results.

Enlist All Members

If you've managed to gather a motley crew, that's great, but it's equally important to enlist them in your cause. Shackleton's talent for selecting his crew wasn't the only factor that contributed to their survival. He was also a master at rallying his men around a common purpose. Although that purpose might have started out as fame and glory, it soon became survival, and he enlisted each and every member of his crew in that endeavor. Each man carried out daily duties that contributed to the group's physical survival, but also their morale. Shackleton encouraged fun and games, including dog races, plays, and singing along with a banjo that was spared even when other items were sacrificed. Shackleton's open door policy and famous listening ear meant that he was able to keep skepticism at bay and maintain commitment to their purpose among the whole crew.[58]

Although your team may not be in quite the same kind of predicament as Shackleton's, if you're looking for breakthrough results, it can be equally important to have a common purpose to rally around. Moreover, each team member should understand how their contribution supports it. You can't realize the benefits of diversity if those differences aren't voiced, so you need all members to be committed to bringing their unique viewpoints to the table. When different perspectives are offered, a group is more likely to examine an issue from multiple sides and pay attention to more sources of information. Psychologist Charlan Nemeth has found that a dissenting opinion can have a positive effect even if it's inaccurate, because dissent broadens our thinking and stimulates originality, and consensus keeps thinking narrow.[59] But if a team member with a different perspective doesn't share it with the group, that perspective can't help others explore or shift their own thinking. If someone who sees a unique solution doesn't suggest it, the rest of the team may never think of it. When an individual disagrees but doesn't say so, their disagreement challenge the team to examine their assumptions or clarify their arguments. Diversity unexpressed is potential unrealized.

Beyond having a clear, shared purpose, one of the best ways to enlist team members and encourage them to share their perspectives—especially those that may go against the grain—is to create a culture that supports *getting real*, which we'll discuss in the next chapter. People who don't feel they can truly be themselves may cover up their unique ideas and perspectives along with their identities. By contrast, an inclusive environment that values different perspectives can enhance feelings of belonging and inspire sharing. (See the *get real* chapter for more help with creating that kind of environment.) When teams are united by a shared purpose and people are confident that it's okay to be themselves, more members are likely to share those unique perspectives. If, however, some are still reluctant, you can encourage them by making it their job to do so. Just as Shackleton assigned his crew specific duties to contribute to each other's care, you might ask team members to take on the role of adding a new, different perspective to what the team is already considering. Maybe one person will be assigned to focus on potentially negative long-term implications and another on the short-term. Or one team member might be asked to represent a customer point of view, and another, a regulator point of view. There are endless options—choose some that are most likely to get new ways of thinking into the mix.

Barriers to Breakthrough

69% of the people we surveyed said the likelihood of expressing what they're thinking may be diminished if they're not sure their input is welcome.

80% indicated they may hesitate if lots of people are talking at once, and **54%** if the conversation is dominated by a few people.

It may not be enough to invite diversity into the room. **Enlisting a motley crew** means creating an inclusive environment that makes space and makes clear that everyone's input is welcome.

Row Like a Crew

Picture for a moment Shackleton's crew rowing a small boat. Now picture them rowing out of sync—maybe the men with the most physical strength are on the left side and those with less are on the right. What happens when the people on one side of a boat are rowing faster or harder than those on the other? The boat goes in circles, that's what happens.

Suppose your own team is quite diverse but people seem to be having difficulty rowing together or seeing eye-to-eye. Although teams that bring diverse perspectives together should, in theory, enjoy the many benefits of diversity, such teams can fail to thrive. Some shuffle along, not producing anything truly innovative, and others get caught up in conflict, miscommunication, and misunderstanding. Diversity doesn't always lead to positive outcomes when people's preferences and needs conflict.[60] If some people on your team prefer directness and others diplomacy, or some prioritize practicality and others creativity, it can be difficult to work together. When people have different ways of approaching problems, making decisions, interacting, or communicating, the potential of diversity can get buried under the avalanche of challenges it brings.

If breakthrough is what you're after, your team will want to emulate an elite rowing crew. Not only must they agree on what direction they're rowing in, but they must also learn to work across their differences to ensure everyone is rowing together.

To understand how well your team is set up to do so, consider your working norms. Often a team works in ways that support some styles—usually those in the majority—more than others. If you want people to offer alternatives to the majority opinion, you'll need to consider whether the ways in which you work truly support that. So, a team with a lot of risk-takers, for example, might not leave space in their timelines for assessing risks and considering downstream implications. If one or two members has a balancing, more cautious orientation, they may not have the opportunity to save the team from big mistakes, because they don't have the time and space to conduct the due diligence they want to. Likewise, if your meetings have a rigid structure, that might discourage sharing imaginative ideas, or if you set team members up to compete against one another, it might interfere with building trust.

Getting your crew to row together means asking yourself whether you're working in a way that can support preferences for challenge and connection, flexibility and discipline, creativity and practicality. Consider whether and how your team encourages respectful disagreement or debate and the extent to which your ways of working might elevate some perspectives and squash others. Look to align your working norms with what you hope to get out of a team, or better yet, balance them to enable a diversity of perspectives to arise.

Looking for practical ways to boost your breakthrough thinking by *enlisting a motley crew*? Jump ahead to our *enlist a motley crew* methods. We'll guide you through the steps to reveal your superpower, assess your team's diversity, mind the gap, interrupt cascades, and celebrate slogans.

Bottom Line Benefits

Enlist a Motley Crew

- Expands the perspectives on a problem as well as potential solutions
- Encourages voicing of dissenting opinions, which broadens thinking and stimulates originality
- Increases creativity, improves problem-solving and decision-making
- Reduces bias by leading teams to pay attention to more diverse sources of information
- Boosts critical thinking, encouraging team members to examine issues more thoroughly and articulate thoughts more clearly

Breakthrough YOU

Enlist a Motley Crew

Do you have personal board of advisors whom you depend on to help you navigate work and life? Do you regularly get guidance from your friends or colleagues? Maybe you ask your parents or siblings for advice? Or do you rely on mentors or a paid coach to help you find your way? Even if you have a clear view of where you're going and how to get there, it can be helpful to have people to cheer you on and provide different perspectives if you get stuck. Anyone you speak with could potentially offer a new point of view, but if you're looking for breakthrough in your personal life, you might ask yourself, just how *motley is my crew*?

In January 2022 a social media thread chock-full of helpful life advice went viral. A mother had typed up and shared the advice her five-year-old offered that morning when she admitted to being nervous about a meeting. Among the wisest snippets of advice was this:

"You gotta say your affirmations in your mouth and your heart. You say, 'I am brave of this meeting!', 'I am loved!', 'I smell good!' And you can say five or three or ten until you know it."[61]

He followed up with an equally astute observation, "Even if it's a yucky day, you can get a hug," and then he suggested you should "Never put a skunk on a bus," which seems like sound advice to us.

All too often people look to the usual suspects for guidance. Although there's nothing wrong with that, consider where else you might find wisdom. What advice might your kids offer? Or your local barista? Or your landscaper? A truly diverse board of advisors would have experiences and mindsets that are different from yours. So consider whom you might add to your own crew to raise its level of motley.

Enlisting a Motley *Business Chemistry* Crew

At Deloitte we use *Business Chemistry* to understand and work across differences. Perhaps more than any of the other Breakthrough Manifesto principles, when you're looking to *enlist a motley crew*, it's immediately apparent how a *Business Chemistry* lens can be powerful. If your team is well balanced across Pioneers, Guardians, Drivers, and Integrators it will, by definition, have a diversity of perspectives and is likely to be highly imaginative and especially rigorous, with strong momentum and excellent collaboration. That sounds to us like a promising recipe for breakthrough.

Business Chemistry is a helpful lens through which to explore whether your team's working norms truly enlist diverse perspectives, as opposed to favoring some over others. Keep an eye on whether your efforts to engage some types might turn others off. Your goal should be to balance the needs and preferences of everyone.

Give **GUARDIANS** the time and the details they need to prepare for a discussion or a decision. Then allow them to contribute in ways that are comfortable for them (for instance, in writing) and that don't require them to fight for the floor— because chances are, they won't. Making advance reading and preparation an option rather than a requirement will lessen the burden for those uninterested in spending time this way, such as Pioneers.

To elicit **PIONEERS'** ideas, allow room for discussions to get expansive. Provide whiteboards and encourage people to get up and grab the marker. Determining in advance how long you'll allow such discussions to go on will help those who prefer more structure—particularly Guardians—to relax into the free-flowing exercise.

For **INTEGRATORS**, dedicate some energy toward forming real relationships on the team—and then ask for their thoughts. Also seek, and empower them to seek, the perspectives of other team members and stakeholders. Explore with them how the discussion or decision affects the greater good. Doing some of this work offline may prevent Drivers from getting antsy with what they may see as time-consuming niceties.

For **DRIVERS**, keep the pace of conversations brisk, and show clear connections between the discussion or decision at hand and progress toward the overall goal. Consider introducing an element of experimentation or competition—say, gamifying a training program— to keep them interested and engaged. Some styles, such as Integrators, may be less motivated by competition, so also look for ways to build or strengthen relationships—for instance, by providing opportunities for competing teams to socialize together.

We're not suggesting that *Business Chemistry* is the *only* lens you should use when considering whether your team has a good diversity of thought—ideally you'd consider other frames for diversity as well. But a *Business Chemistry* lens is a great start for imagining what it can look like when you bring a motley crew together.

———————

GET REAL

Shed the glossy veneer and bring your
authentic, gnarly, bruised, human self.
Magic happens when we're
personal, connected, and real.

Copyright © 2023 Deloitte Development LLC. All rights reserved.

When you're at work, are you a professional or a person? You'd probably like to think you're both—we know *we'd* like to think so—but what you've likely been taught about professionalism may sometimes feel incompatible with being fully yourself. The result for some can be a whole host of behaviors that boil down to hiding aspects of who one is and what one is experiencing in life. Some people act confident or speak with certainty when they're unsure. Others bury their emotions or smile through pain. Some might cover up mistakes, or hide illnesses and pregnancies, looming divorces, and family tragedies. People may pretend to be extroverted even if they're introverted, or say what they think is expected rather than what they *really* think. Sometimes people tone down their personal style or alter how they speak, pretend things don't matter, even when they do, or pretend to care about things when they don't. When asked how they are, even if they're not so good, people usually respond with, "I'm great, thanks, how are you?"

It seems many people may think succeeding at work precludes being their fully human selves. And yet, this kind of pretending, hiding, and covering can have all kinds of negative impacts on the quality of relationships, on levels of engagement and commitment, and ultimately on the productivity and creativity of teams.[62] To generate the kind of creativity that leads to breakthrough, it helps to embrace your own humanity, and that of your teammates, too. Teams can benefit when people bring their unique perspectives out into the open, are willing to offer up ideas before they're fully baked, and risk being wrong. They can often get more creative when people are okay with not being perfect—in fact, a lot of failure happens on the way to breakthrough, whereas playing it safe will likely keep things right where we are. Instead of hiding who you are behind who you think you should be, *get real*. In other words, share more of your authentic self, and risk being vulnerable.

That may seem like a tall order. When we asked 9,000 professionals whether they apply each of these 10 Breakthrough Principles on their own teams, *get real* came in dead last.[63] That doesn't mean it's not worth the effort. Indeed, it could mean there's even greater opportunity in it. But when it comes to *getting real*, it can be a bit tricky to find the right balance between what you share and what you keep to yourself, between who you are and who you might aspire to become, between your own comfort with being authentic and everyone else's comfort. To do so effectively on your team, find your own equilibrium, be yourself but keep evolving, and get real together.

Stories from the Field

Get Real

A few years ago, an executive came to the Deloitte Greenhouse at a pivotal time in his career. He had already ascended and achieved more than most, but he wasn't sure what to do next. As our team asked him questions and guided him through various frameworks, it didn't feel like his "what's next" picture was getting any clearer. The lead facilitator asked him a direct question, "What do you really want to do right now?" In the face of that question, he shared a crucial truth.

He had recently experienced a personal tragedy, and his true "what's next" questions were not about his business self. They were about his human self. The real, grieving one. In the face of a question, this person courageously shed the facade of a perfectly buttoned-up titan of industry. He cried. He *got real*. He was not just an executive, but a person, and he wanted his next steps to matter personally.

With this transformative truth on the table, the executive had space to talk about what was truly important to him without hiding behind a veneer of "doing fine." By *getting real*, he gained clarity of direction. He decided to leave behind his current role and the others he had been considering to accept a top position in his company's health care division. His own experience of tragedy motivated him to improve the experiences and outcomes of individuals and families dealing with health crises. For him, this was a transformative adjustment of purpose and one he was only able to take by being honest, vulnerable, and real.

Find Your Equilibrium

With all this talk about getting real, you might be starting to wonder just how real you should get. Are we suggesting you share with your colleagues your deepest darkest secrets? The short answer is no. And yet, there are no clear-cut guidelines for just how real you should be—it will depend on many factors, including who you are, the norms of the environment you're in, and what you're trying to accomplish with your sharing.

Not everyone is equally comfortable being themselves at work. Some people are by nature more reserved, some have particular identities that they may feel pressured to cover, and some work in environments that don't make them feel safe or compelled to share. This sense of safety is the essence of inclusion, and although many workplaces have worked to strengthen their inclusion efforts over the past several years, it seems fair to say that there's still progress left to be made. A study first published by Deloitte in 2013 found that 61% of respondents were covering at least one of their identities as work.[64] A follow-on study conducted in 2023 found that number had dropped just one percentage point, to 60%.[65] Although anyone might be affected by this tension, concern about whether it's okay to bring their whole selves to work may be more salient for some people than others. The identity categories people were most likely to cover included age, religion, race/ethnicity, mental health status, gender, sexual orientation, current socioeconomic status, and education level. And covering was more common among marginalized groups; however, it was far from absent even among those who identified as white, male, or heterosexual—in each case more than half of those who claimed these identity categories reported covering at least one aspect of their identities. The reasons for covering ranged from hoping to avoid judgments and negative stereotypes to wanting to be seen as competent and suitable for advancement to protecting one's job, physical safety, or mental health.

One result of a less than fully inclusive environment is that expectations about what some people think it means to be "professional" can make it feel particularly uncomfortable to share aspects of oneself that fall outside those bounds.

Inclusion Defined

"The actions taken to understand, embrace, and leverage the unique strengths and facets of identity for all individuals so that all feel welcomed, valued, and supported."[66]

Our own Deloitte Greenhouse research suggests that introverts may be more reluctant than extroverts to truly be themselves, perhaps because they sense their style is less valued in the workplace.[67] In her book *Quiet*, Susan Cain describes the *extrovert ideal* as a tendency for society to place higher value on charisma and outspokenness than on character and reserve.[68] So *getting real* in the workplace may be something introverts view as a bit risky.

A much-discussed *Harvard Business Review* article from 2021 explores another angle on this issue. In this article, Ruchika Tulshyan and Jodi-Ann Burey challenge people to stop telling women, and in particular women of color, that they have *imposter syndrome* when they feel like they don't belong.[69] They aren't imagining they don't fit in, the authors claim, their true selves actually *don't* fit others' expectations of how professionalism in the workplace is often defined. Tulshyan and Burey put it this way: "The answer to overcoming imposter syndrome is not to fix individuals but to create an environment that fosters a variety of leadership styles and in which diverse racial, ethnic, and gender identities are seen as just as professional as the current model."

Fears about sharing more of oneself can be well justified, and each individual should find the level of authenticity that feels right for them, given their environment and context. We're not suggesting you throw every scrap of caution to the wind and let it all hang out (even if you feel totally comfortable doing so). But most people have plenty of room to stretch a bit in the *getting real* department, so we're also not suggesting you just stick with what you've always done. Instead, we recommend you consider whether there might be an opportunity to get just a little bit more real than you or those in your environment typically do. In the *check your edge* chapter we discuss some ways to think about your comfort zone, finding the edges of that, and then expanding those edges a bit. When it comes to *getting real* in the pursuit of breakthrough, it might help to do so by focusing on the types of sharing that are most likely to contribute to breakthrough thinking.

You may recall our discussion in the *enlist a motley crew* chapter about the power of bringing together people with different perspectives, and how creating a culture where people feel they can *get real* supports them in voicing those perspectives. If you're looking to get a little more real yourself, consider sharing more about your perspectives on the world and the problem you're trying to solve, and maybe even the life experiences that have formed your perspective. Sharing your opinions and ideas before they're polished, or before you've made sure they're "smart," can often help move your team forward quickly, especially if other team members take the opportunity to build on your ideas. And as we'll discuss in the *don't play "nice"* chapter, thoughtfully saying what you actually think rather than what you think you should say can be one of the most valuable things you can do to help your team break through to a new way of thinking. (But as we discuss in the *silence your cynic* chapter, it's important to consider the *when*, *why*, and *how* of what you share). When you offer up a bit more about the reasoning behind what you think, it can make an even greater difference.

Another significant opportunity to help your team by sharing more of yourself comes when you make a mistake or fail. The idea of highlighting your own mistakes may feel counterintuitive or even threatening. Many people may feel ashamed of their failures or fear repercussions. And some individuals or groups may feel outsized pressure to succeed based on their identities or may feel failing reflects poorly on themselves and possibly their broader identity groups. But to reach breakthrough, teams must be willing to try things and fail, to take risks and make mistakes. And when you're willing to call out your own failures and mistakes, it can make doing so feel less risky to others.

Talking about your emotions can also be a meaningful way to *get real*. Although some people are taught that emotions have no place in the workplace, they are part of being human, and they can also contribute to breakthrough. Research has shown that being open to the full breadth and depth of your emotions, a state known as *affective engagement*, is a better predictor of creativity than IQ.[70] Moreover, denying your feelings can intensify them, whereas being open to emotions, exploring them, and accepting them can help shift and dissipate them more quickly. It's important to note here that *expressing* emotions is different from *acting them out*. Although it may be helpful to share with your team that you feel frustrated by a lack of progress, for instance, acting brusque and slamming things around is likely to be less so.

Be Yourself but Keep Evolving

If thinking about revealing more of your true self leads you to wonder "Who am I anyway?" you're not alone. One thing that makes *getting real* a bit complicated is that many people don't have a clear idea about just who they are. Do you even have a true self? That's up for debate. There are vast literatures on identity, personality, the self, self-concept, ego, and other related topics. It's fascinating stuff, but you don't need to delve deep into any of that to *get real* in the way we mean. We're just talking about revealing more of what feels like the authentic you. No need to overthink it.

At the same time, it's important to recognize that who you are doesn't have to limit who you can become. *Getting real* doesn't mean you can't benefit from trying things out, even if they aren't what you'd naturally do in the moment. For example, smiling even when you're not feeling it can actually make you happier, jumping in to start something even when you're not motivated can create motivation, and reframing feelings of nervousness as excitement can make you more confident.[71] Likewise, acting as if you're creative, even if you don't think you are—jumping in to *make a mess* as we'll discuss in the next chapter—can actually lead you to become more creative, or at least to be more open to other people's creativity.[72] None of these actions mean that you're trying to be someone you're not; instead, they are examples of how *doing* can contribute to *becoming*.

Sometimes you need to stretch into a role you're hoping to eventually grow into. Professor Herminia Ibarra has written about how getting too focused on who you are could get in the way of becoming who you want to be. The *authenticity paradox* means that applying your own image of who you are in new situations can limit you.[73] She emphasizes that it's okay to "try out new stories about yourself, and keep editing them, much as you would your résumé." *Getting real* shouldn't mean you have to stop evolving.

Many people have aspects of themselves that they're actively working on developing—that they think will make them more effective at their jobs or help them become better teammates. Indeed, a primary tenet of *Business Chemistry* is that it's easier to create powerful relationships with colleagues when you flex your own natural style to better match what others want and need. If you're more reserved, it might not feel natural or authentic for you to speak up in a big meeting, but it could benefit you and the team to do so. On the flipside, if you tend to dominate discussions, it could help you and the team if you experimented with talking less and listening more. As we discuss in the *enlist a motley crew* chapter, teams are more likely to reach breakthrough when they create environments where more people contribute.

Getting real is not an excuse to say whatever you want, whenever you want, however you want, especially when you're working on a team that's chasing breakthrough. It doesn't mean you can just say "well, this is me; deal with it." You need to be able to work with others and get along while *getting real*, which means being in some level of agreement about how to approach things. In the *silence your cynic* chapter we suggest putting your skeptical thoughts to the side, at least temporarily, and in the *strip away everything* chapter we suggest doing the same with your expertise. In the *don't play "nice"* chapter we'll address speaking honestly, but with care. These tensions between what might be natural inclinations and what's beneficial for breakthrough are part of what can make *getting real* feel complicated, but making the effort to find the right balance will be worth it for the benefits it brings.

Get Real Together

In our experience, a fully engaged team is more likely to reach breakthrough. Among the most powerful drivers of engagement is the quality of relationships among people working together—feeling someone cares about you as a person and even having a best friend at work can affect how much effort and enthusiasm you bring to your job.[74] But how can you develop such relationships if you're not being yourself?

Team environments where people feel safe enough to *get real* are characterized by more trust between teammates, stronger relationships, and other benefits, too. A Deloitte study found that professionals who don't feel the need to cover up their identities at work felt a greater sense of belonging and commitment.[75] Other research has shown that people can put more attention to the work at hand when they're not concerned about how they appear to others, and that being part of a team where one's unique perspective is recognized contributes to intrinsic motivation, a key ingredient for creative problem-solving.[76]

So, there is ample reason to encourage authenticity on teams, and yet, building a culture where people are willing to *get real* with each other is no simple feat. Because not everyone is equally comfortable being equally themselves at all times or in all settings, how do you find the right balance between sharing your true self and encouraging others to do the same, but not making people uncomfortable? Some keys to doing so are to share, to ask, and to listen, all while paying close attention to how people react and being ready to pivot if it doesn't feel right.

You might start by setting the example, keeping in mind the types of sharing that are most likely to contribute to breakthrough on your team. Taking a risk and sharing something about yourself might inspire someone else to do the same, and this kind of mutual authenticity can build trust. Daniel Coyle, the author of *The Talent Code*, calls this a vulnerability loop, and he emphasizes that the vulnerability comes first, then the trust, not the other way around.[77]

Barriers to Breakthrough

80% of the people we surveyed shared that a lack of trust may deter joining into team discussions.

73% indicated that they're inhibited if they don't feel a sense of belonging, and **76%** if it seems they can't be themselves.

When people truly feel part of things, they're more likely to take a risk and put their ideas out there. **Getting real** and encouraging others to bring more of their human selves to work is a powerful way to build trust and belonging on a team.

You can then get curious and ask questions that encourage others to share. Sometimes people may want to *get real* but are unsure whether others are interested or how to go about offering up such information, or even whether it's appropriate in the workplace. You can help by asking questions, while being careful not to push too far, too fast, and paying attention to comfort levels—there is a line between getting curious about someone and overstepping into intrusiveness, and it is important not to make others feel obligated to share information that they'd prefer to keep private. Consider questions such as, "Who has had a relevant life experience that might offer helpful perspective here?" Or "Would you tell us a bit more about where your viewpoint comes from?"

The good news is most people actually love talking about themselves. (Even introverts!) Research shows it makes people feel good, lighting up the reward centers in the brain.[78] This is one of the reasons that you may need to make a concerted effort to listen to others—there's often a strong drive to interrupt and talk about oneself—but it also highlights why your relationships can benefit when you get curious about someone else. When someone gets to talk about themselves because you've gotten curious and encouraged them to *get real*, they will likely associate that rewarding feeling with you. And although people are likely to share deeper information with you if they like you, they're also more likely to like you when they've shared deeper information with you. It's a reinforcing circle. Just remember there's a difference between nudging people to be a bit vulnerable, which might be just what they need to get there, and pushing, which is likely a step too far.

Then, of course, if you've asked a question, it's crucial that you actively listen. Too often people are focused on responding, rather than understanding what's being offered. Make eye contact, focus your attention on the person speaking, and ask follow-up questions. When you listen attentively, you can earn more authentic sharing in the future, and as we've already established, more sharing can lead to breakthrough.

Looking for practical ways to boost your breakthrough thinking by *getting real*? Jump ahead to our *get real* methods. We'll guide you through the steps to start a vulnerability loop, flag highs and lows, explore trust, ask deeper questions, and listen.

Bottom Line Benefits

Get Real

- Enhances a sense of belonging and commitment—a result of not feeling compelled to cover up one's identities

- Builds trust and strengthens relationships among teammates

- Super-charges motivation, driven by the sense that one's perspective is recognized and valued

- Normalizes mistakes and failures, which are key to reaching breakthrough

Breakthrough YOU

Get Real

Emotions are a key part of being human. Despite their complexity, many people have a rigid view of emotions, seeing them as good (e.g., joy, contentment, or hopefulness) or bad (e.g., sadness, fear, or anger), and often rejecting those seen as bad, fighting them, pushing them away, denying them, or attempting to tamp them down. Not only is this the opposite of *getting real* but also it doesn't work very well because emotions that are ignored tend to get stronger, a phenomenon known as amplification.[79] Moreover, emotions are a visceral signal that there's something important happening worth paying attention to.

Susan David, author of *Emotional Agility*, has said that "Discomfort is the price of admission to a meaningful life."[80] So instead of pushing them away, she says you must learn to accept all your emotions—even those that feel messy or difficult. Allowing emotions in and exploring what's spurring them can lead to its own kind of breakthrough.

You can adopt a more agile view of your emotions by following David's suggestions:

1. Get curious and explore what the emotion is telling you. What's important about what you're feeling now?

2. Detach from the emotion. Instead of thinking "I am sad," gain some distance by thinking "I'm noticing that I'm feeling sad." You are experiencing the emotion—you are not the emotion.

3. Act from your values and goals rather than your emotions. What's most important to you? Let that guide your behavior.

Stop perfecting and just
start making, doing, trying.
A prototype is worth a thousand discussions.

Copyright © 2023 Deloitte Development LLC. All rights reserved.

CHAPTER

07

If the dictionary were to host a popularity contest among its tenants, the word *mess* would be unlikely to win many awards. As a noun it's something dirty, untidy, confused, and full of difficulties. It's something to be avoided, cleaned up or swept under a rug, or approached with great caution, as in "Careful, that situation's a hot mess." As a verb it's not much better; it's meddling or interfering with something, or fooling around, often with implied negative consequences. As Al Capone's character expresses in *Untouchables*, when people mess with him, he's gonna mess with them.

Culturally, the concept of mess in its various forms is typically considered undesirable. Yet research on creativity as well as our work in the Deloitte Greenhouse has shown that being willing to mess with things, to *make a mess* as our principle advocates, is a critical aspect of breakthrough thinking.[81] Indeed, it seems even working in a messy environment can help promote novel ideas.[82] So how can you stop shunning mess and instead harness it as a force for good?

Let's start by digging into why mess holds such a negative place in many people's minds. After all, kids usually don't have a problem with mess. They are often the sources of it and they revel in it, while adults look on indulgently. Build the tower of blocks, then knock it down and giggle. Dump the entire box of Legos looking for the one blue square. Make mud pies and get covered in dirt. Mess is intrinsic to discovery and learning, and a key aspect of play.

But at some point, as people grow older, that kind of messy tends to become less and less appealing. Things change from "Oh, look how cute" to "Go clean up your mess" because play itself is relegated to a childhood diversion, with productive purpose instead taking its place. The focus shifts from the process (building and knocking down towers) to the outcome (a completed tower). The older one gets, the more mess is seen as unwelcome, even offensive. Over time people may internalize a belief that mess is disruptive, that it's imperfect, that it's uncontrolled, and that it's somehow a threat to the status quo (which humans have a bias toward, as we've mentioned). *Making a mess*, in short, is to be avoided.

As an adult progressing through life and career, these beliefs can be particularly problematic. With your "adulting" hat on, you may tend to aspire more to order, logic, clarity, everything as it "should" be. You may want it to appear that you've got the answers, that you know the "right" way to do things, that you've "got it together," and that you're on a straight path to the goal line, not mucking about on the field. And certainly you're not wasting time playing around. Ironically, these inclinations can hamper rather than help your actual performance—particularly when it comes to breakthrough.

Stories from the Field

Make a Mess

Experiments and prototypes encourage engagement precisely because they're not perfect. The messiness shows that there is room to shape and improve it.

We once worked with a cooperative company looking to refine its future consumer engagement strategy based on member input. They had created a microsite that summarized their research and laid out four possible emerging use cases, beautifully illustrated with artist renderings. They featured the site on digital boards in member locations and actively requested feedback. Several weeks after it went live, however, they had seen only limited engagement.

As an experiment, we decided to run a low-fidelity alternative. In the same locations, we took the research shared in the microsite and laid it out on giant foam core boards, and pinned up paper with "starter ideas" in place of the polished use cases. We provided colored markers and sticky notes, with instructions to add, edit, or eliminate anything on the pages. And we made a few edits and adds ourselves so that the information was already marked up.

Member engagement was almost immediate. Nothing was precious, nothing seemed set in stone, and people felt encouraged to contribute. Whereas in the first example, even though people could have in theory made edits to the microsite (it was shown on an interactive digital board), it felt "finished" and less open to new contributions. Our revised process was messier, but more productive and at a significantly lower investment level for both time and resources.

So what to do? You can try to *strip away everything* and question your assumptions about mess making, and you can *silence our cynic* to be open to the possibility that mess is not a bad thing. But perhaps the quickest path to embracing *make a mess* is to reframe it as something you can get your adult mind behind—practical experimentation. This framing is all about advancing something from the conceptual realm to the concrete, it's about "seeking and blundering" as von Goethe said, in the service of learning more. *Making a mess* is about trying something out rather than just talking about hypotheses or potential solutions. To apply this socially acceptable version of mess making in the service of breakthrough, we suggest you produce a prototype, cocreate, and build for buy-in.

Produce a Prototype

Imagine you're tackling a hairy challenge. You have some ideas but are not sure how to proceed. At this point, you could bog yourself down in endless theoretical discussions, or you could spend some time doing additional research, but we'd argue you might be best served by building a prototype. Derived from the Greek language, *prototype* means "primitive form." It's a method of quickly bringing aspects of an idea to life in a way that enables you to test assumptions and gain new insights through intentional experimentation.

Suppose, for instance, that you want to redesign a showroom or rework a production line. Actual changes would require significant time and investment, but what about a quick and dirty mock-up? We worked with one client who took over an empty hotel ballroom and used cardboard shipping boxes to create a rough layout of their new concept. They then brought in customers and key stakeholders to walk through the space. As people gave feedback, they could respond and adjust things in real time. The room was truly a mess, with stacks of mismatched boxes constantly being repositioned. But within a week they were able to test key aspects of their approach as well as identify several new possibilities—something that would have typically taken months and significant investment.

This example was quite physical, but those inclined toward a more high-tech version of prototyping can consider digital twins. Digital twins are virtual representations of physical things, where the two can be linked so that changes in the one are reflected in the other, and vice versa. Picture for instance that you have a chocolate factory. You make a variety of delicious flavors, but you have an issue where sometimes the nuts and sprinkles versions accidentally mix in with the topping-free options so that, similar to Forrest Gump, you never know what you're gonna get. You suspect that there's a better way to package the chocolates that will keep the different flavors separated. To actually make this change on the factory floor would require significant cost to reposition and reprogram the machines and train the operators. With a digital twin though, you would have a virtual factory that represents the physical model. Experimenting with that virtual model, you could explore the effects of different modifications and make a virtual mess without the expense and potential negative impact of a physical one. This digital twin approach can be great especially when you don't just want to experiment a single time but anticipate ongoing and perhaps quite complicated experimentation.

The concept of prototyping, whether physical or digital, is helpful not only to develop and refine a concept but also to provide a safe place for people to try new things—an essential aspect of breakthrough thinking. A great take on this can be seen in the movie *Ocean's 11*. [Spoiler alert if you haven't seen it: this example reveals the "how in the world did they. . ." secret.] The group in the film plan to rob a casino vault. In order to do this, they construct an accurate, full-scale model of the vault layout. The mock vault, however, is not the thing they're trying to prototype. They're trying to prototype their approach for the robbery. Using the model, the acrobat in the team practices emerging from his hiding place and flipping himself from perch to perch without setting off the alarms. He does this again and again, quite unsuccessfully. He overshoots his mark, he hits the cabinet and slides off, he flubs the landings. In short, he makes a bunch of messy attempts. That practice, however, enables him to adjust his approach, and enables the team to refine their assumptions and ultimately pull off their bold (dare we say breakthrough?) plot. Achieving breakthrough requires not only conceiving of and refining the daring idea but also building the muscles (literally or figuratively) to bring that idea to life.

And although it's great when a prototype provides evidence of what is likely to work, perhaps even more valuable are those that demonstrate what's not likely to work—the prototypes that fail. James Dyson, for example, created more than 5,000 prototypes of his bagless vacuum cleaner before he finally got it right. Imagine the mess *that* made. When he was interviewed by *Fast Company* magazine, he said, "We're taught to do things the right way. But if you want to discover something that other people haven't, you need to do things the wrong way. Initiate a failure by doing something that's very silly, unthinkable, naughty, dangerous. Watching why that fails can take you on a completely different path."[83] So prototyping isn't just about trying what you think will work. It's also trying things that are not likely to work.

You don't need to be a bank robber or product designer to use prototypes to help you experiment. The key is to create an experiment that lets you put your theories into practice, ideally in a minimum-viable format (i.e., messy, not perfect!) that lets you learn and iterate quickly.

An entertaining example of the power of prototyping is the now infamous Spaghetti Marshmallow Challenge and the associated Tom Wujec TED Talk "Build a Tower, Build a Team."[84] The challenge involves tasking teams of four to create the tallest possible freestanding structure using spaghetti, tape, and string. The one requirement? A marshmallow has to be on the top.

Most executive teams doing this challenge spend a long time debating various approaches and discussing possible strategies. "Maybe we need to construct a base foundation that can support a tower." "Maybe we need to support the marshmallow with spaghetti buttresses off each side." What these teams don't typically do, is start playing with the spaghetti and the marshmallow. This in contrast to teams composed of children given the same challenge. The kids dive right in, sticking spaghetti into the side of a marshmallow and then trying to stand it upright. Straight out of the gate, they are hands on experimenting. As a result, the kids consistently outperformed the executives. The process of early, messy experimentation let them quickly try and discard unsuccessful approaches and iterate on perhaps less predictable but ultimately more successful alternatives.

Cocreate

Think back to the days of childhood messiness again, for a moment. What happened when you introduced more kids to the mix? Likely more mess, but also more creativity. That mud pie suddenly became a bakery of mud goods, or sustenance for a metropolis of Muddites, or . . . you get the point. The same thing happens with *making a mess* as adults. Having more adults brings more mess, but also a greater likelihood for breakthrough.

Take for example a session we hosted to help executives understand technology trends shaping the future and envision potential opportunities beyond the horizon line as a result. We created five physical "design dens" with some provocative facts, snapshot "headlines from the future," and key technology inputs. Each of the five teams was given the mandate to cocreate their own technology-enabled future world including thinking through what's valued in that world, who has the power, and where the key uncertainties lie.

Using low-fidelity materials, they worked together to build out key aspects of that future inside their design dens, and then developed a specific market opportunity to pitch to the rest of the group. In less than two hours, we had walls strewn with sticky notes and artifacts, posters pinned to tents, and five diverse opportunities that sparked fresh thinking and revealed underlying assumptions.

This kind of cocreation is a bit like a physical form of the "Yes, and . . ." improv technique we discuss in the *silence your cynic* chapter. It's messy by design and the main benefits are found through the journey and through people working with one another. It was by really diving in and playing with different aspects of their world that these participants got to breakthrough ideas, and the curated chaos boosted energy levels and spurred deeper engagement. The parallel process across the five design dens was also powerful here, providing cocreation at the team level, but also cross-team as the groups compared and contrasted ideas.

Cocreation is even more powerful when it incorporates aspects of play. As we acknowledged previously, play isn't something that's necessarily encouraged for adults, yet it provides a significant boost to the creative process and break-through thinking. Play has been shown to release endorphins, improve brain functionality, and stimulate creativity.[85]

But what is play as an adult? Play is really anything enjoyable that frees your mind, or as Dr. Stuart Brown from the National Institute for Play states, "Play is state of mind that one has when absorbed in an activity that provides enjoyment and a suspension of sense of time. And play is self-motivated so you want to do it again and again."[86]

Although play is powerful for an individual, it has a compounding effect in a group—enriching the experience and building connection and trust.[87] It can help you *get real*. And although it may make the cocreation process messier, the end result will likely be more novel and certainly more fun.

Imagine for instance that you have two groups, each tasked with developing a new operating model for their organization. The one team is given a neat template and asked to work together to figure out the structure, accountability, governance, and other critical aspects of people, process, and technology. The other team is asked to play a game in which instead of the template, they're given challenges—barriers and boosts—related to each of the operating model elements.

Both teams are likely to have a messy discussion as they cocreate together. Both will likely explore divergent ideas and have exchanges and debates about varying approaches. But the latter team, by virtue of playing a game, will be more likely to come at the topics from a fresh vantage point, to explore both serious and "silly" solutions free of constraints, and to engage more deeply with both the content and one another to get at truly breakthrough ideas.

Build for Buy-In

Often when trying to sell an idea, people put great effort into perfecting what they're going to say. With theoretical concepts, though, even a polished pitch may not be enough to get buy-in and alignment. Either the idea at that level sounds inherently compelling, such as the classic "motherhood and apple pie," so there's nothing really to discuss. Or the idea sounds too far-fetched and unrealistic and those cynics (featured prominently in the *silence your cynic* chapter) won't give it serious consideration.

But just like a picture is worth 1,000 words, so too is an experiment. An experiment or prototype pushes you to take something theoretical and make it tangible. When you create something—a mock-up, rough representation, or testable hypotheses—suddenly you're pushing that concept downstream and giving it form. Now rather than debating whether or not something is a good idea, you can see it (or at least aspects of it) in action. It provides a solid basis for dialogue, to increase understanding and ensure you're on the same page with the rest of your team. Why do you choose this versus that? What would it look like if we did *x* versus *y*? How about we try that out and see?

An idea made real in some form, even a messy one, can also be more emotionally compelling. When the director of *Moulin Rouge* was looking to cast some of the best actors in the business in his film production, he didn't rely on the script alone. Instead, he built a small mock-up of the set, and had the actors meet him within that world. That immersion in his vision gave them a glimpse of all that the movie could be and inspired them to commit to the project.[88]

You don't necessarily need a Hollywood-level production to socialize your idea, however. One of our favorite approaches is to create a simple two-dimensional mock-up that enables people to interact with the concept and get a feel for how it would work with zero actual functionality. Imagine for instance that you want to redesign a customer registration system. You could sketch out what the customer sees on a piece of paper, complete with rectangles for the "buttons" the customer can choose to press. When your prototyping "customer" pushes a button, you add another layer of paper reflecting their action, perhaps expanding a drop-down box of options, or bringing them to a brand new page. This approach provides a wealth of information with minimal investment. Not only are you testing out the functionality and gathering real-time feedback from the customer but you are building everyone's understanding of the idea, and the potential extensions of the idea, as you go. And although some might shy away from sharing such a messy, low-fidelity model with their actual customers, if you do have them participate in the exercise rather than just using insiders as proxies, you could potentially get the added benefit of increased loyalty and connection to your product and brand.

Looking for practical ways to boost your breakthrough thinking by *making a mess*? Jump ahead to our *make a mess* methods. We'll guide you through the steps to go marshmallow!, make a metaphor, immerse yourself, stream your consciousness, and draw it out.

Bottom Line Benefits

Make a Mess

- Brings ideas to life quickly through prototypes

- Tests assumptions and allows for rapid iterations of ideas

- Provides opportunities to enrich ideation while building trust through cocreation

- Taps into the power of play in terms of enhanced creativity and engagement

- Makes it easier to get buy-in and creates momentum and motivation to tackle bigger aspirations

Breakthrough
YOU

Make a Mess

We have a colleague who loved art and the idea of painting, but had never tried to paint anything herself because she felt she lacked talent. Her family and friends encouraged her to take an art class, but she was intimidated by the idea of trying to create a work of art in front of others.

Her personal breakthrough came about when her son had a school painting project that when completed left *lots* of leftover paint on the palette (her son was an exuberant paint tube squeezer). Never one to waste things, our colleague decided to use the leftover paint to touch up a vase that she had. She enjoyed layering on the colors with no real plan or picture in mind, simply having fun with the process. After the vase, she kept going, decorating a bird house (also a school project) with colorful stripes and swirls.

The baby step of starting to paint something, anything, in what she admitted was a quite messy process, was enough to boost her confidence and motivation to go further. She signed up for an art class that she continues to enjoy to this day.

If you tend to wait to feel motivated before getting started on things, consider flipping that order. Particularly when you're venturing into new realms and bumping up against our own personal barriers, simply taking a first step can make a huge difference in actually creating motivation and momentum. In his blog "Life Advice that Doesn't Suck," Mark Manson calls this his "Do Something" principle.[89]

Even the smallest step can help you overcome inertia, and the feeling of progress you experience can generate motivation. Part of the power of this approach is not only taking action, but intentionally acknowledging that that action might not be perfect. That it might even be messy. And that's great when it takes you on a path to breakthrough.

_____

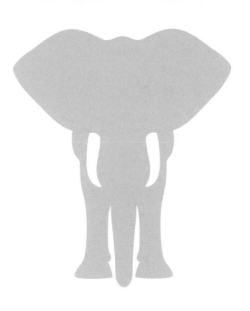

DON'T PLAY "NICE."

Call out the elephants.
The sooner you get truth on the table,
the faster you get results.

Copyright © 2023 Deloitte Development LLC. All rights reserved.

CHAPTER

08

Imagine that you chime in with an opinion during a team discussion and suddenly there's a loud screeching noise and everyone goes silent, the lights dim, and a spotlight shines directly on you. That's what it can feel like when you speak up to say something that contradicts others, when you give tough feedback, or when you call out an elephant in the room.

If you're unfamiliar with the "elephant in the room" phrase, *Wikipedia* provides a useful definition: "a metaphorical idiom in English for an important or enormous topic, question, or controversial issue that is obvious or that everyone knows about but no one mentions or wants to discuss because it makes at least some of them uncomfortable or is personally, socially, or politically embarrassing, controversial, inflammatory, or dangerous."[90] *Wikipedia* identifies the original source of the phrase as an 1814 fable by Ivan Krylov entitled "The Inquisitive Man," about a man who notices all kinds of little things at a museum, but doesn't notice an elephant in the room.

It can be tough to call out an elephant, state a contradictory opinion, or offer feedback that may be hard to hear. It's often much easier to stay silent, to soften a conviction, to agree and go along with the crowd. Instead, we implore you, *don't play "nice."* Speak the truth, even when it's difficult.

The language here is important. We're not suggesting it's wrong to be a nice person. We're huge fans of kindness. To *play "nice"* is to pretend to agree when you don't. To withhold feedback. To let important things go unsaid for fear of ruffling feathers. These common behaviors can mean your team is working with an undercurrent of unspoken opinions, perspectives, contradictions, and conflicts that should inform your problem-solving, but that left unsaid can keep you from reaching breakthrough. To encourage more honesty on your own team, strike the right note, make it worth it, and anticipate differences.

Strike the Right Note

Author Kim Scott's *Compassionate Candor* model (originally called *Radical Candor*) illustrates two reasons people play nice: *ruinous empathy* is holding your tongue because you're afraid of hurting someone's feelings, and *manipulative insincerity* is keeping quiet out of a desire to fit in.[91] Although this model was originally developed in the context of providing feedback, it works equally well for considering whether and how you'll be candid about other issues on your teams.

Most people have occasionally told a white lie or stayed silent with the intention of sparing someone's feelings. "No, your new haircut doesn't make you look like a bowling pin." "Yes, the soup you made is absolutely delicious!" You might sometimes trade complete honesty for these kinds of untruths because you don't want others to feel bad, and perhaps even more important, you don't want to be the one to make them feel that way. In an effort to preserve and protect your relationships, you may decide you're willing to let a loved one stick with an unskilled hairstylist while you endure oversalted soup. Even when people *don't* have a relationship with someone they skimp on honesty; one recent study found that fewer than 3% of participants informed an experimenter that she had lipstick or chocolate on her face.[92] The researchers who conducted that study (and several others) concluded that most people underestimate how much others want their feedback, which can mean that those efforts to protect someone's feelings or avoid awkwardness actually do them a disservice.

Other times people go along to get along; you may keep things to yourself or nod your agreement because you're worried about being excluded from the group if you don't. For many, this behavior was perhaps in starkest relief during high school. "Yeah, that teacher [who is secretly my favorite] is *the worst!*" And yet, if you're honest with yourself, you probably haven't left this tendency completely behind in your younger years but instead carried it into adulthood. "Sure, I'm happy to go to lunch at your favorite sports bar again [even though I think the food is terrible]." Sometimes it feels more important to be part of the crowd than to voice your disagreement about something mundane.

When the stakes are higher, however, such insincerity can be costly. A team member may lose their job because no one was brave enough to share feedback that might have helped them improve. A leader's overbearing style may lead to brain drain on a team because those with the most creative minds would rather leave than raise the issue. A business may fail because it went down a path that the team knew was perilous, but no one was willing to say so. Keeping your thoughts to yourself under these circumstances can hurt your teammates and the team's efforts to reach breakthrough.

Although we're urging you not to *play "nice,"* we're suggesting you should be honest, not mean. As important as speaking the truth can be, this is not a license to be a jerk, what Scott calls *obnoxious aggression*. The goal isn't to create an environment where people feel at risk of being attacked. The ideal tone, from Scott's perspective, is *compassionate candor*. And we agree. This is honesty delivered with caring. When people are willing to engage in honest debate in a respectful tone, a team's problem-solving efforts can start to get more creative.

In the *get real* chapter we talk about vulnerability loops, in which being vulnerable leads to trust, which encourages more vulnerability. *Not playing "nice"* involves a similar loop. By offering your teammates honesty delivered with caring, you can strengthen your relationships, and with stronger relationships you can encourage more honesty.

Stories from the Field

Don't Play "Nice"

We conducted a lab with the marketing leadership team of a large pharmaceutical company whose chief marketing officer had just departed without a clear succession plan. Although the session was ostensibly about re-invigorating their marketing strategy, it quickly became clear that in the absence of the CMO, the company was essentially operating with five different CMOs jockeying for power in a sort of "chief marketer hunger games." No real conversation, much less strategy, could proceed in that environment.

So rather than *playing "nice"* and continuing with the planned agenda, the facilitator mustered up her courage and said to the group, "We can keep going in this direction, but we're not going to get anywhere. It seems like the real issue here is the lack of clarity about leadership and roles after your previous CMO left. If we call that out and talk about that, then we can actually make progress."

Did the team walk out? Did they start battling one another to become the next CMO? No. After a moment of quiet, they affirmed her assessment and then mutually agreed to address that challenge. This explicit acknowledgment of the elephant in the room helped them resolve a festering challenge that had seemed off limits and too uncomfortable to address. They could then get to work toward real breakthrough as a team.

Barriers to Breakthrough

69% of the people we surveyed said they might hesitate to offer up thoughts that could make someone else feel criticized.

And yet, **75%** indicated that people not being honest may discourage them from contributing to a discussion.

Further, **66%** said if the environment is tense or someone is being combative, they may be reluctant to speak.

Not playing "nice" means being honest, even when it may ruffle some feathers, but delivering the message with caring so that it's not destructive but is challenging in a supportive and productive way.

Not playing "nice" doesn't mean you need to blurt out every single thought you have in every given moment; we discuss in the *silence your cynic* chapter the benefits of considering the timing of criticism, for example. But if your team is chasing breakthrough, some particular kinds of truths can be important to speak into existence. If you're not sure how to do so diplomatically, when you see something, use this primer to say something. You may notice these examples line up quite nicely with our other principles.

Moments Not to Play "Nice"

WHEN YOU SEE THIS . . . **SAY THIS . . .**

Someone's behavior is squashing the team's creativity.	"Pointing out flaws can be part of not playing 'nice,' but let's hold the constructive criticism until we've given these ideas a little time to breathe."
The team is basing decisions on potentially flawed information.	"Let's take a step back to make sure we're all confident that we're working with accurate assumptions."
The team is rushing ahead without taking the time to clearly define the problem.	"These initial ideas are exciting! Before we get too attached to them, let's take a beat so we can get clear about what we're solving for."
The team is rallying around an idea that's too limited.	"This is an interesting direction— how might we make it even bolder?"
Diverse voices aren't being sought or included.	"That seems like a reasonable direction, but let's contrast it against some alternate views. Who has another take on how we might look at this?"
There's lots of talking and theorizing, but people seem hesitant to actually try anything.	"I'll bet we could get a clearer idea whether this might work if we moved ahead to create a basic prototype."
People are pretending they agree or are aligned, but you're concerned not everyone is actually on board.	"I'm sensing that some people might not be convinced. Would anyone be willing to voice a contrary point of view?"
People's emotions are simmering under the surface and clearly affecting the team's work together, but people aren't voicing how they feel.	"It's natural that there'd be some emotions about something we're all working so hard toward—why don't we pause to acknowledge those feelings before deciding where to go next."
Team members can't see that it's time to pivot or abandon an initial direction.	"All of this made sense when we started down this path, but maybe it's time to admit that we need to change our focus now."

Copyright © 2023 Deloitte Development LLC. All rights reserved.

Make It Worth It

As helpful as sincere honesty can be, it can often feel risky, especially if the relationships on your team are not particularly strong, the environment lacks robust psychological safety, and/or you're not personally in a position of power. A person who perceives danger in the act of voicing a contrary opinion or calling out an elephant is unlikely to do so unless they have reason to believe it's worth the risk. To understand how this calculation often works, a second conceptual model is helpful here. *Exit, voice, loyalty, neglect* (EVLN) is based on the work of economist Albert Hirschman, and it proposes that people are more likely to take such a risk if they feel committed to the group and if they think it will actually make a difference (i.e., they feel a sense of control).[93]

The EVLN abbreviation represents four ways that an individual might respond to an unsatisfactory situation or a problematic issue. If they don't feel committed to the team or organization, they will likely either leave (exit) or stay but reduce their effort (neglect). *Exit* is likely when a person feels they have control, and *neglect* is likely when they don't, or when they have other significant reasons to stay. Both of these behaviors have been spotlighted in workforce trends over the last several years. The *great resignation,* which occurred in the wake of the COVID-19 pandemic, was an example of exit on a mass scale, whereas *quiet quitting*, popularized in the media in the fall of 2022, was an acknowledgment of widespread neglect. It's an understatement to say that neither of these is good for teams or your efforts toward breakthrough.

However, when commitment is high, *loyalty* is likely if control is low, and *voice* when control is high. Although loyalty sounds like a positive stance, in this case it represents staying in the situation but not actively trying to improve things—in other words, *playing "nice"*—an attitude that's unlikely to contribute positively to breakthrough. If there's something keeping the team from working at its best, what you really want is voice—*literally* for people to voice their concerns.

Our own research supports this model. We asked 28,000 professionals about what prevents them from contributing to team discussions, and more than three-quarters indicated they'd be less likely to share ideas and opinions if they didn't feel committed to the group or if they didn't think the discussion would make a difference.[94]

In order to get people offering feedback, expressing their honest opinions, and pointing out elephants, you'll likely want to focus on increasing commitment, enhancing feelings of control, or both. You might increase commitment through any number of efforts. Maybe you'll focus on building trust by getting to know each other personally, as we discuss in the *get real* chapter. Or you could work on positioning team members to play to their strengths and then recognizing people for their contributions in the ways that are most meaningful to them.[95] Or you might spend time as a team exploring the connections between the team's purpose and individuals' sense of personal meaning.

You might enhance feelings of control by setting the example and tone yourself, pointing out in a respectful and caring manner problematic issues that you see. You can share with your team expectations, techniques, and guidance on the differences between compassionate candor (*not playing "nice"*) and obnoxious aggression (coming off as combative). You could ask that people let you and/or the team know when they suspect there may be an elephant lurking, especially if it's gaining girth. You can respond to such efforts by thanking people for the risk they have taken and doing whatever you can to address the issue immediately. Or commit to doing so at a later date and following up as appropriate. If you can't address it, explain why that is, at the very least. Finally, you might want to share stories publicly about issues raised by others that were addressed or resolved as a result (you don't need to reveal *who* raised it, if it's confidential) and how the team and/or organization benefited.

Anticipate Differences

Numerous factors can affect how challenging or risky it feels for an individual to be candid. For example, the relative authority or power associated with one's position on the team is likely to matter, as is the extent to which one represents a minority perspective. Moreover, willingness to be honest when it's potentially awkward will likely be influenced by individual factors such as level of comfort with directness, tension, and conflict. Here's a place where *Business Chemistry* can make a big difference. Let's imagine you're in a meeting and there's a lively discussion happening. About halfway in, a tiny elephant with disproportionately big ears wanders into the room and plops itself down in the middle of the table. As it sits, it begins to grow.

Maybe a Pioneer is speaking at the time, and everyone is pretty engaged. The Pioneer is very enthusiastic and excited about what they're saying. They don't even notice that an elephant has ambled into the room. If they saw the elephant, they might say, "Holy cow, look, an elephant!" But their focus is on their new idea, and they just keep right on going.

An Integrator may be the first to notice the elephant, because they're most likely to be scanning the room to get a sense of how people are reacting to things. But they might not say anything about it right away, maybe because they don't want to interrupt the Pioneer who's speaking. Or maybe they're not sure how others will feel about the elephant being there. The Pioneer hasn't mentioned it, maybe because they'd rather not talk about it. No one else has mentioned it either, so maybe it's a sensitive subject. The Integrator doesn't want to upset anyone and stays quiet, but pays close attention to the elephant's rate of growth rather than focusing on the discussion.

A Guardian most likely sees the elephant, too, but isn't sure anyone else sees it; after all, no one is saying anything. The Guardian might think maybe there's a reason no one has mentioned it. Is the elephant meant to be there? Was this part of the plan for the day? (The Guardian checks the agenda and sees no mention of an elephant.) What are the expectations here? Is the group supposed to be acknowledging the elephant or not? Not being sure, the Guardian likely won't mention the elephant, but will be distracted by worrying about how long the table can withstand its increasing weight.

It will probably be a Driver who suddenly looks up from multitasking because some strange force is pushing their laptop off the table and into their lap. Only because their progress has been interrupted do they notice what is now a quite large elephant sitting on the table. The Driver will likely blurt out, "Why on earth is there an elephant in the middle of the table—it's about to collapse! We better get it out of here right away." But how to do so now that the elephant is so large it can't fit through the door?

Although this story is admittedly a bit silly, it illustrates how and why people can leave something unsaid, even when that can obviously lead to problems.

Guardians and Integrators often experience less psychological safety and therefore are more reluctant to share ideas, thoughts, and opinions. They are also likely to be less direct, more averse to confrontation, and more reserved generally, all of which can affect the chances that they'll acknowledge an issue no one else is addressing. And this is particularly meaningful because these quieter types may be more likely to notice the elephant while it's still small and easier to deal with, because those who speak less sometimes perceive more. Creating an environment that feels safe is critical for these types, in particular. Moreover, setting up some structures that make speaking up easier (e.g., asking each team member to identify one criticism) may help.

Pioneers and Drivers both may be more willing to speak up. They may differ, however, in the significance they place on the team environment. Pioneers tend to recognize the importance of a welcoming atmosphere. In a study of problem-solving we conducted, Pioneers were the most likely type to emphasize that solving problems works best when the team environment is one of openness, where people feel safe to share their views.[96] Drivers tend to be willing to point out an issue if they see it, but they might be so focused on achieving a goal that they don't notice what's happening, especially if it's an interpersonal issue getting in the way. Drivers don't always notice others' reactions or discomfort, so they may not realize a problem exists. Sometimes a Driver may have a hard time relating to why others aren't willing to speak up and may underestimate the importance of creating a welcoming atmosphere. Because they tend to be quite comfortable with directness and even confrontation, Drivers may not be aware of how much tone matters to others when potentially difficult issues are raised, or how their typically blunt approach to communication can lead others to feel attacked and to clam up. All of this can occasionally mean that a Driver's style of interaction might become an elephant of its own. Giving candid feedback (with caring!) about the impact of their approach may help Driver's to see the benefit of modulating their tone.

Looking for practical ways to boost your breakthrough thinking by *not playing "nice"*? Jump ahead to our *don't play "nice"* methods. We'll guide you through the steps to save a seat for the elephant; go to extremes; find your Achilles heel; like, wish, and wonder; and frame feedback.

Bottom Line Benefits

Don't Play "Nice"

- Removes barriers to ideation, creativity, and sharing of original ideas

- Clarifies whether the team is *actually* in agreement or just going along to get along

- Steers the team away from dead ends and perilous cliffs; when team members who see something say something, it can protect the team from missteps

- Surfaces underlying disagreements and problematic team dynamics that can cause tense environments and discourage participation

- Improves problem-solving—honest debate in a respectful tone enables more thorough analysis of issues

Breakthrough YOU

Don't Play "Nice"

For many people, playing "nice" can take the form of people-pleasing. Although on the surface, it doesn't sound like a bad thing to please others, taken too far it can end up hurting you and not being all that helpful for whomever you're aiming to please.

Many people make small sacrifices for loved ones. Maybe you go to a party even when you don't feel like it because you promised you'd be there. Or you let your kids split the last piece of chocolate cake and go without yourself. You might make much larger sacrifices, too. Maybe you scrimp and save for years so your kids can go to college. Or you put aside your career to care for an ailing parent in their last months. These acts of service, both small and more significant, can give meaning to your life.

But research has shown that a bit of healthy selfishness—maintaining respect for one's own health, growth, and happiness—is associated with higher self-esteem and life satisfaction, as well as more positive relationships.[97] In addition, studies have found that being communally motivated (i.e., caring for the welfare of others) is associated with better relationships, but only among people who don't neglect themselves.[98] In other words, you benefit from finding a balance between serving others and satisfying your own needs.

Finding that balance can be good for the people in your circle as well. Sometimes when you do too much for someone, you rob them of the opportunity to grow and help themselves. Bringing your child's forgotten homework to school for the fifth time could mean they'll never learn to remember it themselves. Rescuing your brother once again when he invests in another risky prospect might mean he won't conduct the proper due diligence when the next opportunity arises.

Next time you feel the urge to please, help, or serve, do a little bit of cost-benefit analysis first—who benefits and who pays the cost? Doing so could be a breakthrough for you and could place others on a path for a breakthrough of their own.

DIALUPTHE DRAMA

Create a full-sensory theatrical experience.
Emotional narrative journeys are how humans
have made meaning since forever.

Copyright © 2023 Deloitte Development LLC. All rights reserved.

When you hear the word *drama*, what comes to mind? Shakespearean oratory on a curtained stage? Soap operas and crime TV series? Angsty teenager histrionics?

Drama is a huge part of life, sometimes for better and sometimes for worse. But when it comes to work, drama is often shunted into the latter category. When people talk about drama in the workplace, they're often referring to unhealthy politics, dysfunctional dynamics, and undesirable emotion. So why then would we recommend *dialing the drama up*?

Turns out that drama is a critical, often overlooked (or avoided) stimulator of creativity and engagement. Drama, used well, stirs the imagination and grabs people's attention. It goes beyond the rational part of your brain and draws out the emotional parts. And those emotional parts are a force to be reckoned with. In his book *The Happiness Hypothesis*, psychologist Jonathan Haidt introduces the analogy of the rider and the elephant, where the rider is your rational brain and the elephant is your emotional brain.[99] Although it might

Stories from the Field

Dial Up the Drama

In one Deloitte Greenhouse session focused on the topic of homelessness, we humanized the issue by gathering testimonials from homeless individuals sharing about their lives. We recorded these interviews, and rather than playing them as videos in the main room, we had participants go into a darkened side room and put on headphones. They listened to the audio track in the dark. Then we turned on the lights and participants saw that around them were profiles of each of the people they listened to, with photos of their daily lives. By hearing only the audio first, the participants listened more intently. When we then layered on the visuals, many voiced surprise as the images didn't match up with what they had envisioned in their head. The resulting discussion was rich and yielded fresh, impactful ideas.

seem like the rider is in charge, when push comes to shove, the elephant often wins.

To get to breakthrough, you need the elephant and rider to head together in a new direction. You need to tap into emotion to loosen any status quo rigidity and enhance logical processing in order to discover fresh thinking. Emotion can help expand and deepen your perceptions by sparking your imagination and layering intuition into your more analytical processing. It can increase engagement, making you more fully present in the moment. And it increases memorability, meaning that effort spent isn't a sizzle in the pan that quickly dissipates, but rather is a flame that continues to burn over time. To enhance your breakthrough thinking in these ways, *dial up the drama* by taking inspiration from three main theatrical devices: set the stage, immerse yourself, and make 'em laugh.

Set the Stage

Think of your favorite theater production. Mentally place yourself in the audience before the show begins and visualize what you are experiencing. You can likely see an area where the action is taking place, perhaps draped by curtains. Perhaps there are backdrops and stage sets and props. Costumes. Lighting. Music, maybe from an orchestra warming up, maybe from a recording. Perhaps there's the smell of popcorn wafting in from a snack area. Or a flowery scent from a floral arrangement. And what about your location? Perhaps you're sitting in a plush seat with worn velvet, perhaps there's a chandelier overhead that dims when the action starts. Or maybe you're picturing a more modern production: a black box theater with minimal décor, the barest suggestion of scene, and functional folding chairs for the audience. Whether elaborate or austere, these elements are how productions set the tone for their piece—establishing mood, building expectations, and evoking emotions.

In the work world, there's a similar opportunity to set the scene and *dial up the drama* for your team or even just for yourself, although people often fail to take advantage of it. Setting the scene often starts with conscious activation, or intentional deprivation, of the five senses. But in business there's a tendency to focus primarily on sight and sound, and even then, the range and diversity of sensory devices tends to be severely limited. From written materials to conference room décor, from conference calls to meetings to speeches, status quo approaches can be a bit "meh."

What if instead, you set the stage for breakthrough thinking by considering the potential of different sensory elements, starting with the basics? Where are you working, or where is the meeting being held? Inside or outside? Is there sunlight? Are there natural elements? These may seem like matters of aesthetic preference, nice to haves, but research suggests they have a significant impact on creative potential.[100]

Use Common Senses

If you want to dial up sensory activation, put on your producer/director hat and think through your "staging" relative to each of the five senses. Here are some sample questions to ask yourself:

What should people be able to see?

Visuals that bring the content to life graphically or that evoke a metaphor? What about props? Who are the actors and how are they choreographed to interact with the space and one another? Are there areas you want to put a spotlight on?

What should people be able to hear?

Specific conversations? Individual testimonials? Music? Sound effects?

What should people be able to feel?

What furniture choices? Temperature? Dress code? Level of activity (sitting versus moving around)?

What should people be able to taste?

Food that matches a theme? Comfort tastes or unexpected flavors?

What should people be able to smell?

Evocative smells (like home baked cookies)? Memory or attention enhancing scents (like rosemary or mint)?

You can combine sensory elements together to heighten dramatic impact, but you can also intentionally minimize, even eliminate, sensory inputs for significant effect. Note the word *intentionally* here. Simply not bothering to have a plan to activate different senses and ending up in a greige office with elevator music and a plastic plant does *not* an environment for breakthrough make. Rather it's consciously downplaying one or several senses in order to heighten others.

In recent years, there's been a fad for sensory deprivation tanks. The concept was first introduced by a neuroscientist in the mid-1950s as a way to study consciousness by cutting off external stimuli.[101] The tanks are sound and light-proof, and have warm salt water that enables people to float seemingly gravity-free within.

Barriers to Breakthrough

69% of the people we surveyed said being bored can diminish their willingness to engage in team discussions.

Even more said their participation may be curbed if they're not interested **(82%),** they don't think it's important **(74%),** they're distracted by other things **(75%),** or feel their time or energy would be better spent elsewhere **(76%).**

You can't assume people will bring their best thinking just because you ask them to. **Dialing up the drama** can grab people's attention, show them why an issue matters, and get them interested and engaged in the pursuit of breakthrough.

Studies report a variety of potential benefits from these flotation experiences, including enhanced imagination, originality, and intuition.[102] Costs can be significant, however, so you may want to experiment with do-it-yourself alternatives. Even something as simple as dimming the lights, closing your eyes, and listening to music in an otherwise quiet space can be powerful to get yourself into a different state. Think of the impact a movie soundtrack has on your perception of a film. How might listening to Wagner's "Ride of the Valkyries" bring drama, versus perhaps listening to Debussy's "Claire de Lune"? Or the *Rocky* theme song?

Immerse Yourself

Becoming aware of the potential for sensory elements in your environment and using them strategically is a great start to bringing drama. There's an opportunity to dial it up even more though to spur breakthrough thinking.

Think about the theater again. In most theater experiences, your attention is on the stage as the focal point, even though you're aware of things in your periphery as well. Indeed, theaters typically are designed to have audiences settled in comfortable seats under dimmed lights in order to dull peripheral distractions and enable people to more fully focus on the action on stage. That's not always the approach though.

One of the more innovative productions that we've experienced is Punchdrunk's *Sleep No More*, a Macbeth/Rebecca-inspired piece staged in a Manhattan establishment transformed into a faux hotel, where the audience can choose where they go and what they see throughout the six-floor space. Some follow their favorite characters, chasing them down hallways to witness key scenes firsthand. Others wander through decadently decorated rooms, where every detail is considered from art on the walls to letters left in furniture drawers. Each audience member wears a white mask, eerily unifying them with each other in their voyeur capacity while at the same time isolating them as an anonymous entity while they each pursue their own individual journey through the play, all in silence. A few audience members may be pulled aside for unique one-on-one interactions with the "residents"—the actors in the piece—perhaps a dance, a whispered request, or a kiss. All are absorbed into their own permutation of the unfolding scene, some comedic, some disturbing.

Using immersion to *dial up the drama* can stimulate breakthrough thinking in multiple ways. By placing people right into the scene (instead of watching from outside it), you more effectively block out the outside world. You make room, literally, for them to focus on their surroundings and indulge their curiosity. What's happening around me? What's the story here? Is there a deeper mystery or puzzle to solve? Immersion wakes the brain up and starts the gears moving.

Imagine that your team is struggling to prioritize time and resources so that they don't become overwhelmed. You could have an analytical discussion about the different demands facing them, or you could fill a room with objects representing these things—emails, customer escalations, team meetings, and so on—and give them a bag that they can fill, but not overfill. Suddenly the challenge has become real in a very literal sense, making it easier to consider the problem from new angles.

Immersion also shifts people from being spectators to participants. With the depth and dimension of sensory clues to help, they can experience a sort of alternate reality, enabling them to interact with that context more authentically and with richer perspective as an active player, not a passive observer. When you have to help pack a physical bag, like in our prior example, it's easier to have empathy about the challenge itself versus dealing with it at arm's length. And that cynic we talk about in the *silence your cynic* chapter is naturally muted a bit, as by necessity people must assume some validity of the premise to interact with their surroundings effectively. So for instance, if you want people to figure out how to optimize a fully automated restaurant concept (e.g., robot/digital ordering and service versus humans), allowing them to interact with a mock-up of one is more effective than having them discuss the idea as a theoretical premise.

Finally, immersion makes for a memorable experience that lasts far beyond the moment. In talking about *Sleep No More,* Scott Brown from *New York Magazine* describes the effect thus, "The show infects your dreams. I've felt theater overwhelm me before, but until *Sleep No More*, I've never felt it pass through me. It was a lovely evening in hell, one I'll be recovering from for some time."[103]

Such a lingering effect is powerful for breakthrough because the experience remains in the back of your mind, influencing your background processing. Much like when you're trying to recall a word and find success only once you stop actively thinking about it, so too can that "aha" thought spring on you when you're no longer actively tackling the problem.[104]

Off the Shelf Immersion

Just want to get yourself or your team to breakthrough and not have to create an entire immersive stage on your own? No problem. There are a plethora of unique homes and environments for rent on online home rental platforms that can serve up ready-staged inspiration!

Make 'Em Laugh

We might not immediately think of comedy as a way to dial up the drama, but in fact this dramatic form is a potent tool in our breakthrough portfolio. Humor and laughter have been shown to have multiple positive effects on health and well-being. But they can also play a beneficial role in creativity and innovation, and thus in breakthrough thinking, in part due to the effect that humor has on your brain. Humor often uses puns that play on different word meanings or positions things from new perspectives in order to find funny, unexpected outcomes.

The process of making sense of puns or figuring out how perspectives relate connects different hemispheres of the brain, and both requires and fuels divergent thinking.[105] Professor Karuna Subramaniam conducted a fascinating study in which people watched different types of videos and then completed a variety of convergent and divergent thinking tasks.[106] She found that people who watched comedy videos performed better in every aspect of creative problem-solving than those who had watched a horror video or a science lecture.

In addition to promoting helpful brain activity, humor can also create a healthy environment for creative risk-taking. The very act of laughing releases tension, relaxes people, and creates bonds between individuals.[107] Barriers are lowered and psychological safety is increased. This is particularly important for breakthrough that may challenge sacred orthodoxies, or that may face up

A surprising and powerful example of the power of humor to support breakthrough thinking is the use of comedy to defy dictators. Popularized in Serbia and since influencing movements across Ukraine, Georgia, Lebanon, Iran, the Maldives, Burma, and more recently Egypt, comedy became a clever "weapon" for protesters against dictatorial regimes. These protesters used cartoons, parodies, and other comedic devices to shift people's thinking and create non-violent opposition to the status quo in order to effect significant change.[108]

against strong, even hostile, opposition. Humor can make the unknown less threatening and can create an atmosphere of playfulness and comradery that makes it easier to take risks.[109]

Often humor is underused in a work environment because people fear it isn't appropriate. "This is business, it's serious." "We don't have time to joke around." But as Jennifer Aaker and Naomi Bagdonas propose in their book, *Humor, Seriously*, far from being a detractor from work, humor can be an incredibly effective business tool to enhance leadership, build trust, and engender creativity.[110] Of course, just like medicine, comedic practice must be pursued responsibly and with the intent to do no harm (a Humorcritic Oath, if you will).

One of the fascinating aspects of Aaker and Bagdonas's research is that the benefits of humor are gained not just in situations of natural levity but also in more critical moments. In some ways, humor in serious work contexts can be even more dramatic, because it's unexpected. Such surprise and delight provides a jolt of energy to people's brains in addition to comedy's other benefits, which can fuel sustained engagement. The humor doesn't even need to be that funny, according to Aaker and Bagdonas. This is one area where, as long as you're not inappropriate or disrespectful, you get points for trying. So next time you're hoping to spark breakthrough, try out that "dad joke" or make that clever pun.

Looking for practical ways to boost your breakthrough thinking by *dialing up the drama*? Jump ahead to our *dial up the drama* methods. We'll guide you through the steps to kick it around, color me breakthrough, light it up, make a playlist, and be a character.

Bottom Line Benefits

Dial Up the Drama

- Brings the power of the whole brain to a topic or situation, tapping into emotion as well as logic
- Increases attention and engagement in the moment
- Improves memorability so that the activation and engagement lasts longer
- Helps accelerate problem-solving and dampens the cynical voice
- Creates a healthy environment for risk-taking

Breakthrough YOU

Dial Up the Drama

If you were in the workforce since the new millennium, you've probably heard the expression *dress for success*. The original idea behind this concept was to dress in a way that would make a great first impression that will wow potential employers, customers, and colleagues. What's interesting about this expression is that various research studies have shown that what you wear is not only important for how others perceive you but also influences how you see yourself, and thus behave as well.[111]

Perhaps you don't think of clothing as a way to *dial up the drama* for yourself, but think again. Want to tackle a new hobby? Try wearing some of the gear. Want to be more edgy? Try a new look. Altough clothes may not actually make the man (or woman), putting on a costume of sorts to intentionally set a tone can be a bit like method acting. It can help you get into the role and way of thinking so that you can take that next big step or try that next new thing.

Finding Balance

You don't need to adopt the Breakthrough Manifesto principles as a permanent state, nor go to extremes—they are most effective when used at a moment in time.

Silence your cynic
There *is* a time and a place for looking at ideas critically, but first give yourself time to dream, explore, get expansive, and build on ideas before poking holes in them.

Strip away everything
Don't stay in an endless, existential loop of examination, but make sure you're thoughtfully applying scrutiny to validate or challenge assumptions.

Live with the problem
Stick with exploring a problem just long enough to get clear on what you're really solving for.

Check your edge
Push past boundaries but stop short of spinning off into the ether.

Enlist a motley crew
Cognitive diversity can be powerful, particularly when ideating, but expertise and other factors are still valuable.

Get real
Be yourself and also maintain some boundaries—consider why you're sharing something before you share it.

Make a mess
Dive in and play around, create prototypes, experiment, then assess what's working and what's not, and clean things up a bit to move on to the next stage.

Don't play "nice"
No need to be mean in order to avoid playing "nice."

Dial up the drama
Evoking emotion can be impactful, but data and facts still matter.

Make change
Make change when it matters, not just for the sake of it.

Copyright © 2023 Deloitte Development LLC. All rights reserved.

Shatter the plan. Evolve. Make a dent.
Nothing matters unless it matters.

Copyright © 2023 Deloitte Development LLC. All rights reserved.

CHAPTER

10

Even though Steve Jobs, founder of iconic company Apple, passed away more than a decade ago, chances are you've heard a version of his quote about "making a dent in the universe." Originally part of a 1985 interview discussing Apple's culture, the quote has been repeated and interpreted countless times in the popular and business presses.[112]

Often this quote is taken as a call to arms to be more purpose oriented: to do something that has positive resonating impact beyond one's self and one's moment in time. Other interpretations, including that of Jobs's wife Laurene Powell Jobs, emphasize the importance of "manipulating the circumstances" and modifying constraining structures in order to get things done.[113] Both these angles share an underlying truth—a call to go beyond simply having great ideas and aspirations to actually making real change. To borrow another Steve Jobs quote when he was recruiting John Sculley to become the CEO of Apple in 1983, "Do you really want to sell sugar water, or do you want to come with me and change the world?"[114]

We embrace this philosophy with our final principle *make change*, because ultimately breakthrough means not only *thinking* of breakthrough ideas but also actually *bringing them to life*. Although the principles we've explored throughout this book will help prime your mind and catalyze aha moments, getting to breakthrough is a journey not just a moment.

At its core, the breakthrough process is a combination of three things: (1) a recognition of a problem or opportunity relative to the status quo, (2) an idea or insight for how to do things differently, and (3) the actions needed to actually make change happen, which themselves often require change and iteration.

The Breakthrough Cycle

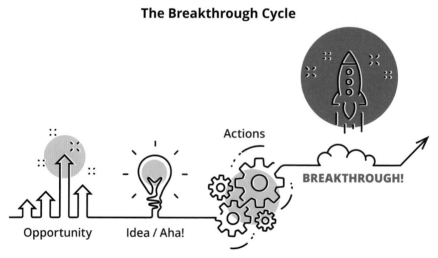

Copyright © 2023 Deloitte Development LLC. All rights reserved.

Stories from the Field

Make Change

We once worked with a company developing a device that could measure a person's mental engagement through sensors placed around their head. The invention was intended to improve training methods by showing when people were paying attention or distracted.

The executives in our session were frustrated because after months of effort and investment it was clear that the prototype was clunky, and although it might work in a laboratory setting, it was uncomfortable and even distracting in a real-life environment.

We took the group through a discussion to rethink and realign on criteria for success for their solution, including a variety of results such as "provides actionable insight on attentiveness" and "doesn't interfere with normal activities." Note that we did not specify the *how* in these metrics (e.g., make the headset more comfortable) but rather the *what* they were trying to achieve (e.g., not disrupt).

The team returned to the prototyping process. They decided to try a different approach that would meet the criteria but come at it from a different angle. They realized that they could correlate engagement levels with other measurable indicators such as heart rate, pupil dilation, and eye movement. They realized the headset device could be used to validate these other indicators but that it did not necessarily need to be the basis of the ongoing solution in the field.

This change in approach let them make leaps forward in creating a way to help people learn more effectively and was specifically targeted toward helping adults in disrupted industries (e.g., coal) quickly retool for other jobs. Now that's a breakthrough that matters.

Although it's often said that humans are creatures of habit, they are also creatures of change—constantly undergoing it and surrounded by it. But that is change happening to and around you. To realize breakthrough, you must intentionally **make** *change*. To make an active commitment to depart from the status quo. To adapt and be agile as the idea evolves. And to make a dent that matters as a result of that effort.

Reframe "Change"

As we mention in the *strip away everything* chapter, humans are not always the biggest fans of change, but often prefer Hobbit-esque lives without disruption. People also have a greater aversion to loss than an attraction to gain, a bias that can significantly color perceptions about change.[115] So to not only tolerate change but also actively effect it, it's helpful to acknowledge your inclinations and reframe the context to aid you in your breakthrough aspiration.

You can start by focusing on the benefits of change rather than miring yourself in concerns about what you might lose. Say, for instance, your company has decided to switch to a hybrid work location model with certain required "in-person" days and the rest of the schedule allowing for virtual work. Perhaps you've been working entirely at home when this change in policy is announced. The loss-oriented mind might say, "Oh no! Do I lose the easy commute from bedroom to desk? Do I lose flexibility in how I get my work done? Do I . . . (dramatic pause) . . . need to stop wearing yoga pants and put on business attire?"

But the breakthrough-oriented mind thinks, "Perhaps I can use my commute to listen to that new podcast series I've been meaning to try. Perhaps now I can optimize my schedule to do independent work on my own, and collaboration and networking when I'm in person. Perhaps I can try out those new kicks I've been wanting to wear and introduce a new business-comfortable fashion trend." The point is, making change starts with changing your own mind about how you view change.

Another powerful way to increase your own and others' dispositions to change is to be transparent about the purpose of that change. Sharing the *why* behind a shift helps provide context and meaning. It creates alignment and can provide a common cause for individuals to rally behind, with the additional benefit of increasing people's comfort and buy-in due to a positive harnessing of the bandwagon effect—the tendency for people to adopt specific behaviors and attitudes because others are doing it. Having a clear purpose will also help sustain engagement typically required to effect lasting change throughout the journey.

Our *Business Chemistry* research also reveals that different styles play a role in how individuals will likely contribute to change efforts, where each may need some help, and what strategies you might use to get them on board.

Pioneers

Pioneers are most likely to embrace big, bold change and to make quick decisions based on gut feel, with only a cursory consideration of the risks. However, more gradual evolution may not feel fast enough for them. Indeed, Pioneers may not be willing or able to stick with a more slow-and-steady change; they're easily bored and prone to switching direction as a result of shiny object syndrome and the proverbial squirrel that may scamper by and distract them. Their flexibility, adaptability, and ability to pivot can be highly valuable, especially in times where rapid change is needed. But other types may sometimes feel Pioneers are making changes just for the sake of change and may view them as reckless. Others may also feel Pioneers have little understanding or empathy for those who are more reluctant to embrace change.

Guardians

In contrast to Pioneers, Guardians likely have an extra dose of status quo bias and may be more comfortable with change by degrees. They tend to deliberate about decisions—it's important for them to conduct due diligence—but once a Guardian decides to start down a path, they'll typically stick with it because chances are that decision was based on extensive analysis. Moreover, Guardians can often foresee the possible domino effects of changes that others may not be aware of. Therefore, they may be reluctant to shift direction if they know it will cause a lot of rework or have other undesirable implications. Although Guardians are often recognized for keeping teams and organizations safe in times of change, other types may also see Guardians as too careful and too conservative, resistant to progress, and frustratingly unwilling to accept any exposure to risk at all.

Pioneer-Guardian: The Power of Opposites

It seems there may be a sweet spot between chasing every squirrel that skitters past and staring down a long string of dominoes. Maybe what's ideal is a balance between the Guardian's tendency to get stuck in a rut and the Pioneer's constant turning on a dime. Imagine a Pioneer-Guardian partnership. It may initially sound like a recipe for frustration, but there is great potential in this combination, especially when it comes to bold changes that present significant risks and also require sustained follow-through. The Pioneer will likely encourage going big while elucidating the considerable rewards that can come from embracing considerable risk. The Guardian will balance the Pioneer's bold approach, outlining potential implications and advising prudent choices.

If a Pioneer is able to get a Guardian on board with a big change, they can be more confident that they are well positioned to make the best of it, having cleared the higher bar presented by the Guardian's caution. They can also rest assured that, once convinced, the Guardian will stay the course to bring the change effort over the finish line. Indeed, in his book *Originals*, Adam Grant highlights research that suggests "our best allies aren't the people who have supported us all along. They're the ones who started out against us and then came around to our side."[116] And "it is our former adversaries who are the most effective at persuading others to join our movements. They can marshal better arguments on our behalf, because they understand the doubts and misgivings of resisters and fence-sitters."

Drivers

Drivers don't usually shy away from change or risk and may enthusiastically embrace both once they've analyzed the key data points. They'll likely support big, fast changes—Drivers are known for generating momentum—but a more gradual evolution can work for them, too, as long as things are moving forward and continuously improving. Drivers are particularly good at making tough choices and don't mind pushing for an unpopular change if they feel it will bring results. Because Drivers aren't prone to either introspection or second-guessing, they'll likely make a decision and move on—their eye is on the prize. This ability to focus can be a strength, but to others, it sometimes looks like tunnel vision. Once a Driver is locked in on a target, it can be difficult to shift their perspective, and other types may experience them as inflexible and unyielding. Moreover, Drivers may roll their eyes at the idea they should build consensus, gain buy-in, or practice diplomacy, and as a result, they may end up driving a bus with no one on it.

Integrators

Integrators, generally speaking, aren't averse to change, but fast changes may not go down well. For them, consensus isn't a nice-to-have, it's a priority, and it takes time to gather input and get people on the same page. As empathic question askers and listeners, Integrators are great at sensing other people's reactions and emotions, and they can be a fantastic resource for understanding what people need in the face of change. Chances are they're also good at communicating in ways that build trust and rally the troops to get behind the change. And they're likely to stay flexible, adjusting their perspective and approach as they consider new information, additional input, or shifting context. But other types may see Integrators as being overly inclusive and taking too long to make decisions because they're trying to make sure everyone is on board. And once they've taken absolutely forever to make a decision that includes everyone's input, the Integrator is still prone to changing their mind. That can feel to others like never getting anywhere.

Driver-Integrator: The Power of Opposites

A partnership between a Driver and an Integrator may be just the ticket for finding the middle ground between an empty bus with faulty brakes hurtling toward its destination and one that meanders aimlessly, picking up one passenger after another until it's overcrowded and overheated. This combination may be especially powerful in the face of a change that's sensitive or initially unpopular, but requires a groundswell of support to succeed. The Driver can be counted on to jump-start the change, make the tough decisions, and push for progress. Meanwhile, the Integrator can be relied on to keep a close eye on how the change affects people, sensing their reactions and needs. A Driver who is very committed to making a change happen will likely benefit from getting an Integrator's help with communicating with sensitivity about the benefits and the challenges it may bring and adjusting the change strategy as required by people's responses. If people follow those they trust (and they often do), Drivers and Integrators together likely have the best chance of getting others on board.

Iterate and Adapt

Most brilliant ideas don't spring into the world fully formed and ready to make their mark. In fact, an original aha is often just a precursor to the final breakthrough. By the time that idea evolves into its polished form, it may be almost unrecognizable. Impactful breakthrough means embracing initial change and ongoing change as well.

Persevere

Sometimes you change things because you must. Maybe your concept isn't working and you need to explore new paths in order to realize your vision. As we discuss in the *make a mess* chapter, James Dyson created more than 5,000 prototypes of his bagless vacuum cleaner before he finally got it right. He wasn't only tweaking things in ways that he thought would be successful but also trying things that were unlikely to work to see what he could learn. History is replete with examples of inventors who kept modifying and adapting their concepts in order to eventually achieve breakthrough. Leveraging the *make a mess* and *check your edge* principles can really help here to fuel different iterations in service of the ultimate objective.

This degree of experimentation can be draining to some and requires a shift from focusing on change as the enemy to change as the agent that will reveal a greater good. As Thomas Edison has been credited with saying, "I have not failed 10,000 times. I have not failed once. I have succeeded in proving that those 10,000 ways will not work. When I have eliminated the ways that will not work, I will find the way that will work."[117]

Self-Disrupt

Although it's sometimes obvious that ideas need changing, that's not always the case. Sometimes as people bring their ideas to life, they form attachments to their own creations. They might fall in love with an early manifestation of their dream and then stubbornly refuse to move beyond it. This commitment can be exacerbated by the sunk cost effect we discuss in the *live with the problem* chapter, whereby one places too much importance on what's already been invested in something and therefore doesn't move on, or the ability of past successes to ensure future success gets overvalued.

To avoid getting stuck in a rut of your own making, you can do two things. First, before you land on any idea, you can lay out desired outcomes that you deem indicative of "success" for your efforts, as well as early signals that you may be headed down a productive path. In order to allow for flexibility in execution, it can help to do this in terms of desirable ranges or threshold points rather than specific data points. So say, for instance, that, similar to Dyson, you have an idea to create a new vacuum system. You could establish several target characteristics that might be integral to a truly breakthrough idea, perhaps things like suction power, weight, charging approach, and so on. You can then use those target characteristics to assess each iteration, and set milestones for where you would like to be performing against those, and potential trade-offs you're willing to make between them. That way you can get a sense of whether you're on track to brilliance, or whether the direction sucks . . . in the wrong way.

Second, you can establish a routine, whereby you regularly apply some of the previous principles to our own thinking. For example, *strip away everything*—what assumptions are you making? *Live with the problem*—are you really solving for root causes versus addressing symptoms? *Check your edge*—are you really going beyond the norm and pushing far enough?

Establishing a regular cadence and habit of applying breakthrough thinking makes it easier to self-disrupt and make change when needed.

Scenario Planning

As we've discussed, breakthrough is more of an iterative than a linear process, and it can also follow multiple pathways versus a single one. Bringing an idea into the world requires shepherding it through multiple future unknowns to keep things heading in the right direction regardless of what variables are thrown into the mix.

Imagine that you're about to parachute into a region as part of an amazing race. From studying a map, you can see that there are three clear routes to your target destination. One is via the desert, one is via the mountains, and one is via water. These three paths each would require quite different approaches, and until you get on the ground, you don't know what local conditions or barriers might impact your route.

In this situation, it can help to think through various possible scenarios and contingency plans. What happens if there's a flood? Or a road is washed out? What are the crossover points between the trails in case you need to change course? If you get lost, what landmarks might help you to course correct?

This kind of option-oriented planning can make it easier to make change in the moment. By anticipating potential disruptions and alternate approaches, you can be far more agile in pursuing, and ultimately achieving, breakthrough.

Make a Dent

Breakthrough requires change to bring ideas to life, but not all changes are breakthroughs. To merit the label, a change must be meaningful. Significant. It has to matter. It can be easy, therefore, to set the bar for breakthrough so high that you hesitate to attempt it. But meaningful change comes in many shapes and forms.

Making change can be dramatic, like a lightning strike, or more subtle, like the butterfly effect: the idea that minute changes in initial conditions can have drastic effects on outcomes. Meaningful changes can be rapid, like the chemical reaction that causes an explosion, but they can also be gradual. Look at evolution: the pace is glacial, but the stakes couldn't be higher. Meaningful changes can result from direct action, like the ripples on a lake's surface that result from a stone being thrown in, or they may result from a catalyst being introduced. Maybe you've heard about the cascade of indirect ecological changes that have occurred since wolves were reintroduced to Yellowstone Park; among those changes, the wolves keep elks on the move, which prevents them from overgrazing on willow stands, which allows beavers to thrive.[118]

Meaningful changes can make things better, but they can also make things worse; which experience you have may depend on your perspective. For example, climate change is likely to spell disaster for penguins, who depend on sea ice for breeding, but may be a boon for jellyfish, who will benefit from an expanding habitat as waters warm.

Meaningful changes can affect multitudes, like the development of a life-saving vaccine, or they can affect just one being. In Loren Eiseley's *The Star Thrower*, a boy is walking along a beach throwing stranded starfish back into the water.[119] An old man observing says, "You can't save them all, so why bother trying? Why does it matter, anyway?" And the boy ponders, throws another starfish into the sea, and responds, "Well, it matters to this one."

There is no one size fits all for breakthrough. But although making change may in some ways be very personal and individual, you do not need to go it alone. Indeed, some of the most powerful breakthroughs revolve on people coming together to make lasting change. This takes a great idea and magnifies it to a level that makes a difference to one, and to many.

Looking for practical ways to boost your breakthrough thinking by *making change*? Jump ahead to our *make change* methods. We'll guide you through the steps to navel gaze, establish rituals, motivate with nudges, plan for scenarios, and find your why.

Bottom Line Benefits

Make Change

- Encourages not only thinking of great ideas but also bringing them to life

- Provides perspective on how to improve your openness to change based on universal human biases as well as individual *Business Chemistry* differences

- Presents an approach for how to iterate and adapt through perseverance, self-disruption, and scenario planning

- Offers a challenge to make a positive lasting dent in the universe

Breakthrough YOU

Make Change

Nelson Mandela once said, "One of the most difficult things is not to change society but to change yourself." [120]

People naturally change and evolve throughout their lives, but it takes a different level of self-awareness and dedication to consciously change one's self. Similar to making change with a breakthrough idea, it can start with a recognition of the current state and identification of where there might be opportunities.

- Is there a delta between your stated goals and your actions, for example, you say you want to live a healthier life, but you keep junk food in your kitchen and skip planned workouts?

- Is there a barrier between what you think and what you say, for example, you hate that your friend makes insensitive jokes, but you laugh politely along instead of speaking up?

- Is there a discrepancy between your world beliefs and your behaviors, for example, you believe in kindness but you're quick to get irritated and snap at others?

Once you identify the gap, now's the chance to be creative about how you're going to address it. It's probably not enough to just say, "I'm going to do something differently." If that were the case, you likely wouldn't have the gap! Instead, leverage the principles throughout this book to push yourself to think differently, challenge your assumptions, and come up with some ideas. Then keep at it. Try different things, adapt and evolve, and most important, don't give up. Get yourself to breakthrough, and make a positive dent in your own world.

Making Change
That Matters

One of our personal favorite examples of making breakthrough change that matters at scale is an organization called Charity: Water that is dedicated to helping bring clean and safe water to every person on the planet by building easily accessible wells. This organization emerged out of an aha insight from Scott Harrison, a former nightclub promoter who realized that he could use his influence for good. He set up a model whereby private contributions would support operating costs, so 100% of public donations could go to helping people in need.[121] And he had some particularly impactful ideas for how to make change. The first was to work with local partners to implement the wells versus constructing them without community involvement, and to establish broader practices to ensure ongoing sustainability of the venture that would work with the resident culture.

The second idea was to create a movement centered on birthday donations. Harrison was able to garner celebrity interest in the concept of reallocating money that would have been spent on birthday gifts and parties to Charity: Water donations instead. Big names donated their birthdays and raised visibility about the cause. But the birthday approach wasn't limited to the rich and famous. Children around the world donated as well, some with personal, heart-rending stories that sparked significant additional contributions. Harrison was able to go beyond a great idea to create breakthrough impact by involving many people to help make that change happen, and he continues to innovate on how he extends reach and long-term sustainability.[122]

BREAKTHROUGH

MANIFESTO

SILENCE YOUR CYNIC

SUSPEND DISBELIEF AND ASSUME EVERYTHING'S POSSIBLE

NO GREAT BREAKTHROUGH WAS BORN OF A NAYSAYER

STRIP AWAY EVERYTHING

SET ASIDE EVERYTHING YOU THINK YOU KNOW

ASSUMPTIONS, BELIEFS, AND DOGMA ARE THE ENEMY

LIVE WITH THE PROBLEM

AVOID RUSHING TO THE SOLUTION

BETTER THINGS COME TO THOSE WHO EXPLORE BEFORE ACTING

CHECK YOUR EDGE

ASK YOURSELF, "IS THIS TRULY UNEXPECTED?"

SURPRISE IS THE MOTHER OF INSPIRATION

ENLIST A MOTLEY CREW

GO BEYOND THE USUAL SUSPECTS

SPARKS FLY WHEN THINKERS, DOMAINS, AND OUTSIDE DISCIPLINES COLLIDE

GET REAL

SHED THE GLOSSY VENEER AND BRING YOUR AUTHENTIC, GNARLY, BRUISED, HUMAN SELF

MAGIC HAPPENS WHEN WE'RE PERSONAL, CONNECTED, AND REAL

MAKE A MESS

STOP PERFECTING AND JUST START MAKING, DOING, TRYING

A PROTOTYPE IS WORTH A THOUSAND DISCUSSIONS

DON'T PLAY "NICE"

CALL OUT THE ELEPHANTS

THE SOONER YOU GET TRUTH ON THE TABLE, THE FASTER YOU GET RESULTS

DIAL UP THE DRAMA

CREATE A FULL-SENSORY THEATRICAL EXPERIENCE

EMOTIONAL NARRATIVE JOURNEYS ARE HOW HUMANS HAVE MADE MEANING SINCE FOREVER

MAKE CHANGE

SHATTER THE PLAN, EVOLVE, MAKE A DENT

NOTHING MATTERS UNLESS IT MATTERS

BREAKTHROUGH
METHODS

Copyright © 2023 Deloitte Development LLC. All rights reserved.

Putting the Principles into Practice: Breakthrough Methods

We believe in breakthrough, but we're also pragmatists. Each Breakthrough Principle is based on extensive experience and research into what it takes to shift mindsets, amplify ideation, and galvanize action. We hope that in reading about these principles you gain significant insight into *why* the principles matter and *how* they might apply to your work and your life. But to push from idea to action, we believe it's important to suggest some options for *what* you might do as well. And that's where our Breakthrough Methods come in.

In the Deloitte Greenhouse, we design and use thousands of different methods to create tailored experiences that help get our clients to breakthrough. These methods are sets of actions in service of a specific purpose; they are the means by which we manifest the Breakthrough Principles. True breakthrough is not only an idea but also action toward positive change. In this section of the book, we've curated a set of methods for each principle, intended to help provide a solid foundation for you and your team to boost your breakthrough thinking and launch toward positive change.

Some of these methods can be useful for both individuals and teams, and others might have a more specific target audience. The methods can be used alone or in combination with one another. We recommend thinking about them like ingredients in your kitchen that you can mix and match differently depending on what you're trying to make. Need to prime your brain? Try a dash of this. Want to generate some ahas? Try a pinch of that. As with cooking, the more you practice, the more you'll develop an instinct for what's needed in any particular situation. Perhaps you'll even start tweaking some of these methods to better suit your tastes or create new, delectable concoctions of your own.

Ultimately, there are many possibilities for how you can use these methods and others to promote breakthrough, so don't limit your thinking to what's on these pages. But whatever you do, do something. Don't let this book live quietly on some shelf. Dog ear your favorite approaches, mark up your observations, loan your copy to a friend, or even tear out pages to use with your team (no, really). It's all good. After all, although we're in the business of getting to breakthrough, how you use this book to get there—that's none of our business.

Best of luck on your journey, and here's to breakthrough!

UNREALISTIC
NO / IMPOSSIBLE
DIFFICULT / BUSY
EXPENSIVE / BUT...
TIME-CONSUMING
WE DON'T DO THAT
I DON'T THINK SO
CAN'T / WON'T
BE REALISTIC
I WISH

How to Boost Breakthrough Thinking by Silencing Your Cynic

There's a wonderful expression from theater about the audience needing to have "a willing suspension of disbelief." To truly immerse themselves and appreciate the story, they need to put their cynicism on hold. This idea of suspension, versus dismissal, is key to *silencing your cynic*. You are pausing the judgment long enough to let fresh thinking tiptoe out from the dark corners, to encourage other voices to add their perspectives to the mix, and to let yourself explore being a problem-solver, not a problem-pointer-outer. At the same time, you are actively resisting potential cynicism around you, so that it doesn't infect you.

The following are a set of powerful methods for helping teams and individuals effectively work to *silence your cynic*.

Silence Your Cynic Method 1: Interrogate Yourself

It's okay, even healthy, to be skeptical once in a while. The key is to make a conscious decision about when to be skeptical or not, to be vigilant in diagnosing the source of that skepticism, and to avoid sliding into the more corrosive space of cynicism.

As we discuss in the *strip away everything* chapter, shedding light on assumptions and biases can help defuse nonproductive skepticism and redirect intellectual fire power to getting to breakthrough. In this case, we're trying to shed light on your own internal processing so that you can consciously mitigate and/or direct your doubt. In essence, rather than focusing your skepticism (and potentially toxic cynicism) outward, we're suggesting first turning your scrutiny inward. After all, as author and astronomer Carl Sagan is quoted as saying, "Skeptical scrutiny is the means . . . by which deep thoughts can be winnowed from deep nonsense."[123]

How to interrogate yourself:

Step 1: Identify what is triggering your skepticism to identify the source of your reaction. Is it an idea? A person or team? A situation? Yourself?

Step 2: Ask yourself, what is it about that trigger that is bothering you, for example, . . .

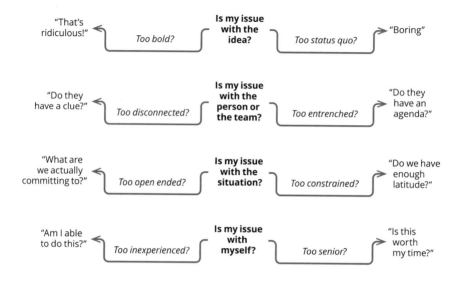

Step 3: Identify the assumptions underpinning the issue. In other words, what is leading you to think something is too bold or too status quo, and so on?

Step 4: Use the *strip away everything* methods (coming next!) to interrogate your thinking.

Step 5: If you remain skeptical, no problem. Just keep in mind *when* you choose to share that point of view (be careful in the early stages of an idea or relationship), *why* you're sharing that point of view (be wary of political or power-based motivations), and *how* you share that point of view (be thoughtful about your tone, phrasing, and audience).

NOTES:

....

....

....

....

....

Silence Your Cynic Method 2: Ask What If . . .

Have you ever been to an improv show, where audience members provide a topic and then the improv actors create a scene in real time building on one another's ideas? If you haven't, it typically involves a random prompt from the audience, such as someone shouting "An alien visits your mother-in-law . . ." and then the actors riff on that, for instance:

"So my mother in law was visited by an alien and now she's convinced they're all around us."

"Yes, and she's set up a neighborhood cosmic watch to flag suspicious activity."

"Yes, and she's been getting so many calls that her phone line is constantly busy."

"Yes, and I guess that means her ET can no longer phone home."

Granted the professional improvisers are generally more talented at improvisation than we are, and actually funny, but you get the point. The thing is that improvisational techniques can be very helpful in promoting breakthrough thinking, and this approach in particular can be useful when you're first trying to solve a problem with a team or group.[124] Many people have a natural inclination to immediately dismiss "out-there" ideas, but you're more likely to reach breakthrough if you instead first lean into the absurd and productively build on ideas. That way cynicism won't kill possibilities straight out of the gate, not to mention the process will likely be more fun.

How to ask what if . . .

Step 1: Begin by articulating the challenge as clearly as possible in a single sentence. Referencing the story we share in the *silence your cynic* chapter, that might be "How can we safely and effectively remove ice from power lines?"

Step 2: Encourage the group to spend a few minutes thinking individually and writing down every idea that comes to mind, no matter how crazy. Share that the intent of this exercise is to generate as many ideas as possible, not to evaluate the ideas for viability, desirability, and so on. To amp up engagement, consider a friendly competition based on number of ideas generated.

Step 3: Ask one individual to share one of their favorite ideas, starting with the words, "What if we . . . [state new idea here]."

Step 4: Ask others in the group to build on the first idea by saying, "*Yes, and* . . . what if we . . . [state idea here]." Ideally these new ideas would be additions or refinements to the original idea and not a completely separate thought. Capture all the emerging ideas visually, for instance, on a digital canvas, whiteboard, or wall with sticky notes. Encourage everyone to participate; if one voice is dominating, invite those individuals not speaking up to add in. Continue until the idea tapers off.

Step 5: Proceed with other starter ideas until you have a good set of possibilities. If you seem to be getting the "usual suspects" of ideas, encourage the group to share their strangest or most outrageous ideas and repeat the process.

Step 6: Ask the group to review the collection of ideas and to vote on their favorites to explore further (you can do this voting anonymously to mitigate groupthink), as well as to capture additional ideas they may have.

Step 7: For the top ideas, ask the group to discuss: What is it about this idea that is compelling? What would it take to make this the best idea possible?

NOTES:

Silence Your Cynic Method 3: Change Your Mind(set)

One way to effectively counteract toxic skepticism is to shift your mindset. The brain is neuroplastic and capable of forming new neural connections (mindsets) at any point in life.[125] The goal here is not to permanently *silence your cynic* but rather to strategically suspend disbelief and doubt, so what you likely need is a *temporary* mindset shift. One way to change your own mind for just a while is to assume someone else's. You can take tips on how to do this from a profession that specializes in it: acting.

Imagine for a moment that you're a method actor, and that you aspire to not only represent a role but truly embody a character. One of the unique aspects of method acting is that actors often choose to live as their character even when they're not on stage or filming, sometimes going to extremes of diet, exercise, and life changes to maintain authenticity of character. They try to draw from personal experiences, either living in the role or from their memories, to get into the mindset of their characters by understanding their emotions.[126]

We're not suggesting you have to make dramatic lifestyle changes for the sake of *silencing your cynic*, but we do suggest trying on a different point of view and coming at it from an emotional and not just intellectual lens. Try playing a part other than "the naysayer" and play it from the heart.

How to change your mind(set):

Step 1: Think about relevant roles for the topic at hand and choose one to play. This role could be something categorical such as "the customer," "the investor," or "the new hire." It could be something descriptive such as "the eternal optimist," "the diplomat," or "the explorer." Or it could even be a specific famous person, such as Richard Branson or Leonardo DaVinci (two of our personal favorites). The point is to choose something very different from the starting, cynical mindset.

Step 2: Consider what the mindset of this role is likely to be:

- What are their hopes? What are their fears?

- How do they feel when faced with a new opportunity? How do they react?

- What are their priorities?

- What experiences or memories do you have that might be similar to this role's?

Step 3: Step into the role. It can help to vocalize this (even if you're by yourself), saying something like "I'm going to play the diplomat now" or "If I were Richard Branson, here's how I might think about this."

Step 4: Proceed to discuss the topic while you stay in character. It's okay (beneficial even) to note where your viewpoint might differ from the role you're playing, but don't let that sidetrack you from an Oscar-worthy performance.

Step 5: Don't flee the stage too quickly, but when you're ready, officially step out of the role (again vocalizing can help, for example, "I'm taking off my diplomat hat now . . .") and then debrief the discussion. This part is about what the role-acting perspective revealed about the topic that might not have been as evident before.

Consider: you don't need to be a one-person show. There's power in asking various individuals on the team to play different roles in order to "borrow" alternate mindsets.

NOTES:

Silence Your Cynic Method 4: Get Physical

Caution: just reading this method may trigger skepticism in some, but bear with us as we've found this approach to be quite effective in maintaining a more positive, less cynical, mindset. The core idea here is that your body can influence your mind. In particular, the way you stand, move, and breathe can affect the way you feel, and can also change the way people perceive you . . . for the better.[127] In this method we'll emphasize one specific approach for doing this inspired by body language expert Patti Wood.[128]

You may have heard about open or closed body language before. Wood's work builds on this concept with an idea she calls *Body Windows*. These are locations on the body that typically represent your most vulnerable areas. When a person is feeling uncomfortable, or exposed, their limbic reactions can lead them to protect these areas by making them smaller or covering them, or to prepare for fight or flight by tensing them. This is called *closing* windows. Not surprisingly, the opposite behavior when people feel comfortable is called *opening* windows.

Closed body windows include postures such as crossed arms and legs, squinted eyes, pursed lips, and hunched shoulders. What's interesting about these body positions is that they not only look closed off but they also can make you *feel* closed off. One study showed that stooped posture activates negative mood and interferes with recovery from pre-existing negativity compared to straight and open postures.[129]

To make things worse, humans sometimes mirror the body language of others, so if you're closed off, you could not only be affecting your own attitude but you also may be affecting others![130]

So to recap: you're more likely to be cynical if you're feeling vulnerable (as we discuss in the *silence your cynic* chapter). You're more likely to close off your body windows if you're feeling vulnerable. And having closed off body windows can increase your feelings of negativity, which could in turn amp up your likeliness of toxic skepticism and potentially influence others to feel that way, too. Sounds like an unhealthy cycle you'd want to break! Here's how to start, by opening your body windows.

How to get physical:

Step 1: Make yourself aware of your current posture and body position. Are you tense? Hunched? Covered?

Step 2: Starting from your feet and moving up your body, actively relax your muscles, uncross your legs and balance your stance, drop your hands to your side, put your chest up and your shoulders back, raise your chin, widen your eyes, and smile. Or at least don't grimace.

Step 3: Breathe—deeply, repeatedly, and intentionally.

Step 4: Repeat as needed throughout the day if you notice yourself tensing up or closing off.

NOTES:

Silence Your Cynic
Method 5: Buddy Up

If you've ever seen Jim Henson's *The Muppet Show*, you'll likely recall two of his iconic characters—Statler and Waldorf—the curmudgeonly hecklers who delight in criticizing the other Muppets' performances from their balcony theater seats. Harsh cynicism is one of their less than desirable traits. So when we suggest "Buddy Up" as a method, we're not suggesting teaming up with a fellow cynic and criticizing to your heart's delight.

But the thing about cynicism is that sometimes people are not aware that their comments or behavior may be moving away from healthy skepticism and/or taking the group down an unproductive path. They can be influenced by unconscious biases, or in the heat of discussion, have temporary amnesia about what we share in the *silence your cynic* chapter, or maybe never even read it, or they can just be in a bad mood. The point is, in spite of your best intentions to *silence your cynic*, there can be many reasons why you might not live up to those intentions. And similar to other good intentions, it can help to have someone else holding you accountable for achieving them.

So forget that cynical Muppet duo archetype, and get yourself a breakthrough buddy instead.

How to buddy up:

Step 1: Think about situations where you are more likely to be cynical. Are there specific "triggers"—topics, people, circumstances—where you're more likely to react negatively?

Step 2: Consider who you know who might be able to observe you in those situations. Note: it is important that this person is someone whom you trust and who would be willing to serve as a buddy. Bonus points if you reciprocate and play this role for them in return!

Step 3: Ask this person to do one of the following:

    A. *Intervene*: Say something if they notice you behaving in a cynical fashion. This can be calling you out directly or simply a code word that signals to you that you should pay attention. You can decide with your buddy what is most comfortable for you.

OR

    B. *Document*: Take note of what was happening in that moment, how you responded, and why they felt you were not effectively *silencing your cynic* in order for you to discuss and debrief later.

Step 4: Consider whether there are common patterns leading to your cynicism. Doing so can help gradually improve your self-awareness over time.

NOTES:

_____

_____

_____

_____

_____

_____

_____

_____

_____

_____

_____

How to Boost Breakthrough Thinking by Stripping Away Everything

Picture shopping for a new house in a very tight market and finding one that hits all the key points of your wish list, is within your price range, and is situated at just the right location. Imagine you go inside and take a look around only to realize that whoever decorated it had very different taste than you. In fact, you hate it. But you're unlikely to find a house that better fits your criteria, so you buy it. Once you own the house, do you just accept and learn to live with the decor? Not likely. You rip down the wallpaper and tear up the carpets to see what's underneath, and then you create a look that suits you.

When it comes to problem-solving, the *strip away everything* principle is kind of like that house. Instead of accepting the beliefs, assumptions, and orthodoxies that are limiting your thinking, consider it an invitation to strip them all away so you can see new possibilities.

The following are a set of powerful methods for helping teams and individuals effectively *strip away everything*.

Strip Away Everything Method 1: Flip Orthodoxies

As we discuss in the *strip away everything* chapter, orthodoxies are pervasive beliefs that often go unstated and unchallenged. One orthodoxy some organizations shared prior to 2020 was that virtual work just wouldn't work for them. This orthodoxy affected real estate and staffing decisions, including who could fill which roles, and who could do what work, when, and where. When COVID-19 led to office shutdowns all over the world, organizations entered an involuntary experiment that forced them into challenging this orthodoxy. Many of them found that virtual work was possible—although not without challenges it could often work. Our own team in the Deloitte Greenhouse was compelled to strip away our long-held belief that we couldn't deliver engaging experiences for our clients virtually. When we had little choice all of a sudden, we put aside what we previously "knew" and applied our energies to figuring out how to do what was needed at the time. We found that indeed we *could* make virtual experiences engaging. This method can help you challenge your own orthodoxies intentionally, even without a global pandemic forcing your hand.

How to flip orthodoxies:

Step 1: Identify your deeply held, shared beliefs. It may be helpful to organize your beliefs in categories, such as *our organization*, *our customers*, *our industry*, and *our competitors* (or some other categories that make sense for you.) Start with the question, *What do we know to be true?*

Step 2: If you're trying to solve a particular problem, identify those beliefs that are directly related.

Step 3: Flip each belief to identify its opposite. For example, the opposite of *virtual work* can't *work for us*, is *virtual work* can *work for us*.

Step 4: Brainstorm what could be possible if the flipped orthodoxy was indeed true. For example, *we could broaden our talent pool by hiring people who don't live near our offices*.

Step 5: If you identify any intriguing possibilities, interrogate the original orthodoxy further. Is it really true? Consider sleuthing for truth (*Strip away everything* method 3) or searching for UFOs (*Strip away everything* method 4).

NOTES:

Strip Away Everything Method 2: Defy Constraints

Constraints are a particular flavor of orthodoxy—what are the boundaries that you're trying to problem-solve within? Likely suspects may include resources (e.g., people, time, money), regulations or requirements, and factors related to customers, competitors, and other aspects of the market. Remember the cynic we discuss in the *silence your cynic* chapter? They can be very fond of pointing out constraints. It often sounds like "That will never work because of *x*, *y*, or *z*." But focusing on your constraints can keep you from exploring what *could be*. Because the world is constantly changing, it makes sense to look past constraints that exist now but may not in the future. Moreover, sometimes the constraints you think you see may not actually be there, such as the belief that consumers would never buy eye glasses or sneakers online. This method can help you get more creative by looking past constraints.

How to defy constraints:

Step 1: Identify the constraints related to the problem you're trying to solve.

Step 2: Imagine one (or all) of the constraints were not there. In other words, imagine an unlimited budget, or unfettered access to the top experts in the field, or customers whose disposable income isn't affected by recession or inflation.

Step 3: Brainstorm solutions to your problem that could be possible if your constraints weren't present.

Step 4: Consider whether there is anything in those ideas that can be applied once your constraints are back in place.

Step 5: Bonus points for using the other methods in this section to interrogate the constraints themselves. Are they really real?

NOTES:

Strip Away Everything
Method 3: Sleuth for Truth

Sometimes you might think something is true because you read about it in a book, blog, or article. Whatever you read may have cited research or other evidence supporting the author's claim. Or sometimes an author cites someone else's book, blog, or article, which cites the research or evidence. Other times, an author makes claims based on anecdotes or without any supporting evidence at all. Or maybe you didn't even read the thing you think is true but once heard someone you respect make the claim. Maybe they said something like "research has shown this claim to be true," but they didn't say any more about the actual research. Maybe they read it on the internet. Or maybe *you* read it on the internet. The point is, a claim can quickly become conventional wisdom or accepted fact, with few people truly understanding what actual evidence exists to support it.

When *we* were in school, our professors emphasized the importance of following the trail of a claim back to its original source—of looking for the evidence or reading the original research reports supporting the claim. Maybe your professors taught you the same. Sadly, people don't always do what their professors instructed.

Maybe you're not an academic researcher and don't have the time, inclination, or expertise to follow a belief or claim all the way back to its original source. We get it. But might you make an attempt to follow the path of a claim at least a few steps backward? After all, it's to everyone's benefit to be making decisions, setting policies, and solving problems based on verified information rather than folklore.

How to sleuth for truth:

Step 1: Identify a key belief related to a problem that needs to be solved or a decision that needs to be made. For example, as we've discussed, prior to 2020 many organizations made decisions about working and meeting locations based, in part, on the belief that virtual work wouldn't work.

Step 2: Ask how you know this belief is true. What's the evidence? Is there any evidence that the belief is *not* true?

Step 3: Go deeper. Explore the source of the evidence. Is it based on personal or professional experience? Data? Anecdotes? Instinct? Published research? Did someone *read it somewhere*?

Step 4: Pressure test the evidence source. How credible is it?

Step 5: If your exploration leaves you less than confident about the original belief, explore how your problem-solving would be affected if the belief were *not* true?

NOTES:

Pressure Testing an Evidence Source

Questions to ask about data:
- Who collected the data? How was it collected?
- How raw or processed is it? Is it heavily interpreted?
- Who analyzed the data? Did they have a particular bias, perspective, or incentive?
- Are any identified differences statistically significant? Practically meaningful?

Questions to ask about published research:
- Who conducted this research and what do you know about them?
- Where was the research published? Is the publication peer reviewed? Reputable?
- Do the study participants seem comparable to those affected by your current problem or situation?
- How large was the sample? Was there a control group or condition?
- When was the research conducted? Has anything significant changed in the world since?
- Have the findings been replicated, challenged, or refuted by other studies?
- **Note:** Research reviews or meta-analyses can provide more reliable evidence than individual studies.

Questions to ask about personal/professional experience:
- Whose experience? One person's? Many people's?
- How deep is this experience? How broad?
- How might cognitive biases affect interpretation or recollection of this experience?
- Has anything changed since this experience?
- Has anyone had contrary experiences?

Questions to ask about what someone *read somewhere*:
- Who read what, where? Can they produce a link or citation?
- Who is the author of the piece, where did it appear, and are both reputable?
- Does the piece cite evidence and include the sources that allow you to track back further?

Strip Away Everything Method 4: Search for UFOs (Unidentified Fact Options)

Once upon a time, even the fastest people in the world couldn't run a mile in less than four minutes. (Incidentally, most people *still* can't!) The world record set by Gunder Hagg in 1945 held steady for nine years at 1.4 seconds above the four-minute mark.[131] At the time, it seemed no one would ever be able to break through the four-minute barrier—many believed it was physically impossible. Then in 1954, Roger Bannister did it, and others quickly followed. It seemed Bannister helped break some kind of psychological barrier that kept times above four minutes and that once he proved it could be done, others were able to do it as well.[132]

This story is sometimes shared as an example of how widely held beliefs about what's possible (or not) can prevent breakthroughs. It's a compelling idea and makes a great illustration. And we happen to believe that psychological barriers *can* prevent breakthroughs. However, in this case, the psychological barrier theory is not the only possible explanation for this pattern of record-breaking miles. Author Steve Magnes has written an alternative theory, namely, that it was World War II that led to the stagnation of running times around the world, and the eventual recovery from the war that explained several runners breaking the four-minute barrier in succession.[133] During the war years, many young men died, were injured, or did not have the luxury to train for elite running events. By 1954, training had modernized and a new crop of men across the globe had matured into peak running age.

Our point here is not that one theory or the other is correct—we're not experts on running or world wars. Instead, we're sharing this story to highlight the concept of illusory correlation. Sometimes the timing of two occurrences leads one to perceive a relationship between them that doesn't exist, without considering the other factors that may be at play. When you explore other possible explanations, it can enable you to consider a problem from a new angle.

How to search for UFOs:

Step 1: Identify the key beliefs related to a problem or decision. (You might currently think of these as *facts*.)

Step 2: Ask yourself what some alternative explanations might be. Although the internet can often be the source of erroneous information, it can also be your friend when it comes to the search for alternative theories and explanations. If someone has an alternate theory, it likely appears online somewhere. But you can use your own brain power to think of other explanations as well.

Step 3: Explore how the alternative explanation would affect your search for solutions.

Step 4: Consider whether there is even a kernel of an idea that you can build on regardless of which explanation is true.

NOTES:

Strip Away Everything Method 5: Reuse and Repurpose

Sometimes people get stuck in a rut where it's hard to be creative, particularly when dealing with a topic or area they know a lot about. One reason that may happen is the phenomenon of *functional fixedness*, which means once you become familiar with the way an object is used—its function—it can be difficult to imagine how it could be used differently.[134]

In a classic experiment demonstrating functional fixedness, psychologist Karl Duncker demonstrated this effect by giving people a box of thumbtacks, a candle, and a book of matches.[135] They were instructed to attach the candle to the wall so that it wouldn't drip wax on the table when lit. Trying to tack the candle to the wall didn't work, and neither did melting wax to hold it there. The solution (spoiler alert!) was to dump the thumbtacks out of the box, tack the box to the wall, and place the candle inside it. If Duncker presented the box and the thumbtacks separately, instead of with the thumbtacks inside the box, people saw the solution more easily, because they didn't become as fixated on the function of the box as a holder for the thumbtacks.

Functional fixedness anchors people on assumptions for how something is supposed to be used.[136] The following is a game that can help your team practice stripping away those assumptions to find new creative solutions and then extrapolate that way of thinking to other breakthrough ideas.

How to reuse and repurpose:

Step 1: Create a set of cards, each with an image or name of an everyday object (e.g., a shovel, a birdhouse, a sock). Alternatively, you can use the cards from a game called Disruptus.

Step 2: Draw a single card from the pile and do one of the following:

    A. *Reuse:* identify as many unconventional uses of the object as possible.

    B. *Repurpose:* come up with a completely different way to achieve the purpose of the object on the card.

Alternatively, draw two cards from the pile, and come up with a new object or idea that combines those two concepts (trying to be as creative as possible). So, for instance, a tricycle and a lightbulb could spark the idea of a set of workout machines (bikes and more) that can generate electricity.

Step 3: Step back from the game and think about what assumptions you're making about whatever your actual challenge or opportunity is that might benefit from this approach:

- What assumptions are you making about how something can be used? What are alternative uses?

- What assumptions are you making about the purpose? Are there alternate purposes to consider? Or different paths to achieving the purpose?

Step 4: Discuss implications for your effort.

NOTES:

How to Boost Breakthrough Thinking by Living with the Problem

When you've got a tough problem to solve, it's natural to want to get right to it, but you might be better off taking a pause first. We're not suggesting you shouldn't take action. If cynicism is the more negative cousin of skepticism, as we suggest in the *silence your cynic* chapter, then avoidance is the lazy cousin of patience. What we're recommending is that the action you take be something other than immediately jumping into problem-solving mode. Spending more time on the problem first could help you sort out whether it's even the right problem to begin with, or if it's worth spending the time, effort, or money to solve for it. Is it worth the investment? Pause to consider whether the problem is actually worth solving and, if so, how much you're willing to invest to solve it. Sometimes you'll find you really are just willing to *live with the problem* forever.

Among our favorite things about this principle is that there is no "right" way to go about it—there are endless ways—conducting research, gathering and analyzing data, visualizing, whiteboarding, mind mapping, deep thinking, and talking to others are all legitimate ways to better understand a problem, and any of these techniques can be applied alone or with others. We're suggesting you *live with the problem* a bit longer, not forever. Set a time frame or a particular level of understanding to be reached, at which point you'll move on to solutions.

The following are a set of powerful methods for helping teams and individuals effectively *live with the problem*.

Live with the Problem Method 1: Act Like a Toddler

Toddlers can be notorious for driving adults to distraction by repeatedly asking the question, "Why?"

"You need to eat your veggies."

"Why?"

"Because they're good for you."

"Why?"

"Because they have lots of vitamins and fiber that make your body strong."

"Why?"

"Oh, just eat your veggies already!"

Although this practice may be a bit annoying in daily life, when it comes to breakthrough this dogged commitment to digging into a line of questioning can be particularly helpful.

In the *live with the problem* chapter, we tell the story of a team that was struggling with high rates of turnover in their organization. When they asked themselves why it was happening, they realized people were feeling dissatisfied. When they asked themselves why *that* was happening, they concluded it was due to feelings about compensation, and also opportunities for growth. In the chapter we highlight how asking (again) why people were dissatisfied with those issues could shed even more light on how to best solve for them. You can go through the same process of asking why, and then asking it again several times, whenever you're trying to understand the root cause of a problem.

How to act like a toddler:

Step 1: Write down the problem or challenge.

Step 2: Ask *why*. (*Why* is it happening? or *Why* is this a problem?) For example, why are people leaving?

Step 3: Answer the first *why*, starting the answer with *Because*. . . . For example, because they're dissatisfied.

Step 4: Ask *why* in relation to the first answer. If the first answer had more than one possibility, create branches, and continue asking *why* about each branch separately. For example, why are people dissatisfied? Because (1) they're unhappy with their compensation and (2) they're unhappy with the opportunities for growth.

Step 5: Repeat three to five times until you feel you have reached the root of the problem or challenge. Toddler tears and other tantrum behaviors optional.

NOTES:

Adding a Little *What If* and *How* to Your *Why*

In his book *A More Beautiful Question*, journalist Warren Berger illustrates the power of going beyond *why* questions, following them up with *what if* and *how* questions.[137] A powerful way to use this question trifecta is to ask

- Why are (or should) things be the way they are?
- What if they were (or could be) different?
- How might we make it so?

Why?

In Berger's own words, "ambitious, catalytic questioning tends to follow a logical progression, one that often starts with stepping back and seeing things differently and ends with taking action on a particular question." He suggests that one of the signals that someone is an innovative questioner is refusing to accept the existing reality. That's the *why are things the way they are* part. And as we've already discussed, *why* is not a question to be asked just once, but many times.

What if?

The *what if* part involves imagining possibilities beyond the existing reality. Berger suggests staying in this fun stage for a while, letting ideas build and percolate. Indeed, he says it's important not to try and answer a difficult question too quickly.

After asking and answering, "*Why* are people dissatisfied with their compensation?" for example, you might follow up with.

- *What if* we paid people enough that they were thrilled with their compensation?
- *What if* our culture was so compelling people cared less about their compensation?
- *What if* we didn't pay people at all? (Think that sounds outrageous? Ask Wikipedia how many hours of labor have been donated to their site!)

How?

If you land on a *what if* that sounds intriguing, ask, "*How* might we make it so?" For example, "*How* might we go about creating a culture that's so compelling people will care less about compensation?" The *how* can move you, finally, toward solutions. The language is important here. The *might* encourages aiming high and exploring possibilities without feeling you're locking yourself into commitments.

Live with the Problem Method 2: Change the Lens

Maybe you're willing to *live with the problem* a bit longer, but you're not sure what you should actually be *doing* with that time. One option is to explore several new ways of looking at the problem. People are used to seeing how the world works from their own perspective. What does it look like from others' perspectives? It can be easy to get attached to a particular vantage point, either seeing your part of something and losing sight of the whole, or missing the trees for focusing on the forest. What happens if you toggle between the big picture and the details? There are multiple sides to each situation. How do things look if you flip the current state around? We offer five options below for changing the lens.

How to change the lens:

Step 1: Determine whether your team has one view of the problem or many. Ask each team member to write down their own succinct summary of the problem you're solving for. Post them up and review them together. Do members have a shared view or many different views of the problem?

Step 2: Look through someone else's eyes. Consider these perspectives:

- *Competitors*: How do/would they view the problem? Are they likely to see or react to it differently?

- *Customers*: How does the problem affect them? How will they benefit from it being solved? What do they want?

- *Leadership*: What do they think the problem is? If they were going to focus on just one thing, what would it be?

- *Stakeholders*: How do they feel about the problem? What are their concerns and what do they value?

- *Those on the front lines*: How do those most directly affected by the problem view it? What would they change or improve?

Step 3: Toggle between the big picture and the details. How can solving the problem benefit individual people, your team, the organization, your community, the world?

Step 4: Fast-forward. To break out of the paralysis of the here and now, fast-forward to a future state. Pick an applicable time frame; maybe six months or six years down the road. What does the ideal end state look like? What is the current trajectory? What are the consequences of your decisions? What is the worst-case scenario?

Step 5: Consider an analogous angle. Often, inspiration comes from applying the lessons of one context to another. (e.g., What can a health care organization learn from a retailer?) Ask yourself, who has faced a similar challenge? Are there lessons to be learned from other industries, countries, or professions?

NOTES:

Live with the Problem Method 3: Try Question Storming

When you're trying to solve a really challenging problem, you'll be more likely to find a great solution if you first ask a lot of questions. And one of the most powerful ways to use questions is to come up with a lot of them, a technique sometimes called *question storming*. The Right Question Institute suggests that it's easier for most of us to come up with questions than with ideas or solutions, and this question formulation technique encourages divergent and convergent thinking.[138] They encourage coming up with 50 or more questions about any particular topic, because the best questions often come after the first, most obvious questions are asked. Once you've got a long list, engage in a process of narrowing down to the most fruitful questions.

Similar to brainstorming ideas, question storming can be done alone or in a group, in person or virtually, at one moment in time or asynchronously.

How to try question storming:

Step 1: State the problem or issue to be explored.

Step 2: Write down as many questions as you can without stopping to discuss, judge, or answer the questions. (Write down questions exactly as stated and turn any comments into questions.)

Step 3: When you feel like you've run out of questions, challenge yourself to come up with 10 more. Then do it again.

Step 4: Prioritize the questions. Which have the most power to reveal something new?

Step 5: Select the top three questions and discuss their possible implications for refining and solving the problem.

NOTES:

Live with the Problem Method 4: Stretch Out Your Brainstorming

Traditional brainstorming usually follows a pretty straightforward process. You announce a topic or problem. People shout out ideas. Someone writes them down and there's no judgment allowed. That's it. These kinds of brainstorming sessions are ubiquitous. This, despite the fact that there is a substantial amount of research indicating that traditional brainstorming, whether virtual or in person, is not the best way to come up with the best ideas.[139]

For one thing, brainstorming in this way doesn't allow for much opportunity to *live with the problem*. The problem is announced, and people immediately shift into problem-solving mode. One incremental improvement to this process could be to announce the problem in advance of the brainstorming session so people have time to think about it for a bit longer before they're expected to come up with solutions. Research suggests that when people are told about an upcoming task but asked to do something else first, they're more creative than when they jump right into the task.[140] And if you announce it at least a day in advance, people will have the opportunity to engage in *live with the problem* method 5 and sleep on it!

Another way to give your team more time to *live with the problem* could be to switch to electronic brainstorming, which can mitigate production blocking (when you can't share your idea because others are talking) and help reduce evaluation apprehension.[141] Electronic brainstorming can also expand the time available for people to both *live with the problem* and come up with ideas. As a result, you could get more, better ideas from a more diverse collection of individuals.

How to stretch out your brainstorming:

Step 1: Announce the problem and identify a dedicated area for the brainstorm on your favorite electronic collaboration tool.

Step 2: Allow people to anonymously submit ideas over a period of several days. If you've *enlisted a motley crew*, you'll see it paying off here in terms of the diversity of ideas offered when you make it safe to do so. Encourage people to return again and again to review others' ideas and add more of their own (but not to comment yet on others' ideas).

Step 3: Move into an asynchronous comment period, also going over several days, during which people can comment and build on each idea.

Step 4: Bring people together (in person or virtually) to discuss and prioritize ideas as well as next steps.

NOTES:

Live with the Problem Method 5: Sleep on It

As we mention in the *live with the problem* chapter, when you've got a compelling problem to solve, your brain can keep working on it even when you're not consciously doing so.[142] This is the idea of *passive percolation* we mention. It really could not be simpler.

How to sleep on it:

Step 1: Put the problem aside.

Step 2: Go to sleep. (Or alternatively, go for a walk, listen to music, take a bath, play fetch with your dog, cook a meal, do *anything* but actively work on the problem.)

Step 3: Pick the problem back up at a later time.

NOTES:

How to Boost
Breakthrough Thinking by
Checking Your Edge

There's an expression sometimes voiced by well-meaning status quo defenders, "If it ain't broke, don't fix it." Apart from the potential downside to this thinking—that innovation will never occur if one intentionally avoids innovating—there is another aspect to this expression that can limit breakthrough potential. And that is the idea that something must be wrong in order to merit change.

While it may be true that breakthroughs can address significant problems, they also can unlock novel benefits. That distinction is key because it means that breakthrough potential is always there. You don't need to seek it out only when there is a problem that threatens your comfort zone. Rather, you should consider making a regular practice of checking your edges, particularly when the status quo is especially comfortable, to see what surprising opportunities might lie just out of view.

The following are a set of powerful methods for helping teams and individuals effectively *check your edge.*

Check Your Edge Method 1: Plot Your Portfolio

Our strategy organization at Deloitte has a simple but powerful framework that positions innovation as a portfolio of efforts aligned with business strategy and risk profiles.[143] This portfolio is categorized by three curves: *core*, which reflects improvement on existing things; *adjacent*, which focuses on expanding into nearby spaces; and *transformational*, which addresses opportunities yet to be discovered. Both adjacent and transformational zones represent edges to explore, with increasing breakthrough potential as the range extends further from the status quo.

So, for instance, if a shoe company invents a new kind of sole, or a more efficient or differentiated way to manufacture their shoe (e.g., 3D printing), that is considered core innovation. If that company begins selling athletic attire and related accessories, that's considered adjacent innovation. If that company then creates an activity tracker and related system to collect data and gamify fitness and health, that's thought of as transformational innovation.

The Innovation Ambition Matrix[144]

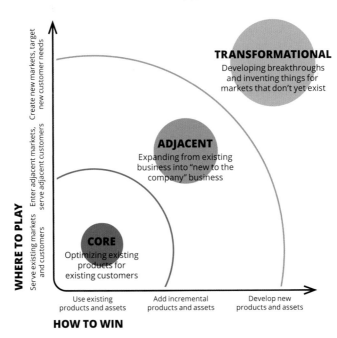

The framework suggests that your efforts should be strategically allocated across the three categories to sum to 100%, where the distribution is typically weighted most heavily in core and least in transformational, but with specifics that vary based on industry and business context. For breakthrough thinking, the emphasis here is less on precisely what the percentages should be in each of the three categories and more on ensuring that the focus doesn't default to core.

How to plot your portfolio:

Step 1: Draw three curves like the previous image, or create three columns, and label them to represent the innovation categories

- Core

- Adjacent

- Transformational

Step 2: Put each of your current, or potential, innovations into one of the three categories.

Step 3: Evaluate the mix:

- Does the portfolio balance reflect your innovation aspirations?

- Are you *checking your edge* sufficiently through this mix?

Step 4: How might you further *check your edge* with this portfolio?

- Are there other adjacencies that could be explored?

- Are there core resources that could be redirected to fund transformational moonshots?

- Why are these the optimal set of innovation choices for your team or organization?

NOTES:

Check Your Edge Method 2: Think Three Bears

Most people are familiar with the story of Goldilocks, for-ever seeking the perfect outcome that's not too much, or too little, but "just right." When it comes to *checking your edge*, a simple technique could be to think about an idea in terms of a three bears spectrum—extremes on both ends, with an average in the mid-dle. Unlike Goldilocks, however, your intent is not to necessarily stop in the middle ("just right"), but rather to explore the implications of being at either extreme. So let's say, for example, that a company has an idea to offer a new technology service to its customers. What if they offered that service com-pletely for free? Or at an unprecedented premium? What if they offered that service only to their best customers? Or to anyone who asked for it? For each decision about the idea, rather than starting where they "think" the answer probably should be, they could instead push themselves to consider other, significantly different, alternatives.

The power of this approach is that it helps loosen the tether of familiar grounds and connects to a novel perspective that provides a different vantage point for exploration.

How to think three bears:

Step 1: Think of an idea or solution you're considering.

Step 2: Reflect on different ways to make that idea more extreme, for instance:

- No fee versus premium fee

- Restricted access versus open access

- No investment versus unlimited investment

- Time bounded (short or specific deadlines) versus timing independent

- Narrow impact versus broad impact

Step 3: Capture each extreme on a different sticky note or card.

Step 4: Mix the cards together into combinations and evaluate them. Which combinations are the most surprising or unexpected?

Step 5: Discuss the implications of these extremes and insights for what "just right" might look like given the conversation.

NOTES:

Check Your Edge Method 3: Play Mad Libs

Mad Libs is a game in which the players suggest arbitrary nouns, verbs, and adjectives to fit into blank spaces in a story, creating a random narrative that is typically silly, nonsensical, and entertaining.

Although intended as a fun distraction for children and adults alike, Mad Libs can also be a useful tool for promoting breakthrough thinking. The process of generating words haphazardly and then seeking meaning in their combinations can be a powerful way to break away from the familiar and explore surprising new possibilities. This method can prime your brain for other creative thinking, but it can also reveal some potential breakthrough ahas as you explore nuances of meaning.

How to play Mad Libs:

Step 1: Take one minute (timed) to brainstorm a list of adjectives, nouns, and verbs. Don't try to filter for what might logically make sense; just come up with as many words as possible in the given time frame. Put the list aside.

Step 2: Develop a starting sentence that makes sense for your situation, for instance:

In order to have a viable solution, the management team must get aligned.

Step 3: Identify the main adjectives, nouns, and verbs in the sentence and rewrite the sentence with blanks in place of the words you've indicated.

*In order to have a **viable (adjective)** solution, the **management team (noun)** must **get aligned (verb)**.*

Step 4: Select one word on your initial list from each category (adjective, noun, verb) and put them into the sentence to replace what's currently there, for example:

*In order to have a **moral (adjective)** solution, the **public (noun)** must **commiserate (verb)**.*

Step 5: Discuss this new sentence. What about it is interesting? Surprising?

Step 6: Continue developing new sentences with the list of arbitrary words. Play with replacing all of the words each time, or just a few.

Step 7: Discuss insights from these alternate sentences.

Step 8: Another variation on this method is to find a compelling combination of words, and instead of switching out the adjectives, nouns, and verbs randomly, try inserting synonyms for those words instead. This can provide fresh insight on the nuances of the sentence.

NOTES:

Check Your Edge Method 4: Mix It Up

Variety is the spice of life, so be intentional about seasoning yours. This method is all about disrupting your daily patterns to intentionally inject novelty into your routine and help stimulate your brain.

How to mix it up:

Step 1: Choose a daily habit where you're almost on autopilot, for instance:

- Brushing your teeth

- Checking email

- Your commute to work

- What you eat for breakfast or cook for dinner

- Scheduling work meetings

- Your television show selection

Step 2: Deliberately change something about your routine, for instance:

- Brush with your other hand, or floss first.

- Read 10 emails before answering any, or vary whether you check email first or tackle a challenging task first.

- Take a different route to work, or ride your bike.

- Change what or when you eat, or try a different venue such as eating outdoors.

- Limit meetings to 20 minutes or take a walk while talking.

- Try a different form of entertainment, such as solving a puzzle or playing cards.

Step 3: Continue to experiment with doing at least one new thing every week. And don't limit yourself to things for yourself. Try injecting some surprise into others' lives through spontaneous outreach and interaction.

Step 4: A variation on this method could be to have your entire team try something new, either choosing the same daily individual habit (e.g., everyone decides to vary their commute to work) or choosing a shared team habit (e.g., the team always meets in a particular team room or always orders lunch from the same place).

NOTES:

Check Your Edge Method 5: Push Yourself

The Last Dance is a 10-part documentary telling the story of the rise of Michael Jordan and his dominance over the basketball world in the 1990s. He started his career as a high-flying aerial specialist, dazzling crowds with awe-inspiring dunks. He kept his edge by spending hours in the off season and in training camp reinventing his style and developing new skills, such as one of his signature moves: the fade-away jumper.[145] This story of reinvention can be seen throughout sports and provides good inspiration for how to *check your own edge*.

How to push yourself:

Step 1: Choose something where you have solid competence, for instance:

- Mountain biking

- Speaking a foreign language

- Spreadsheet wrangling

- Playing tennis

- Public speaking or presentation

- Cooking

Step 2: Think about a novel challenge related to that competency—something that poses an increased level of difficulty for you, for instance:

- Bike riding in tougher terrain

- Taking on a new language or joining a conversation class

- Leaning more complex formulas and data manipulation techniques

- Trying out a new stroke or playing a different game (e.g., doubles versus singles)

- Challenging yourself to speak without notes or slides

- Experimenting with a new cuisine

Step 3: Set a goal that you find a little intimidating related to that challenge.

Step 4: Keep at it, trying to find your flow state where you are challenged enough to feel focused and exhilarated, but not so challenged that you freak out or fail.

NOTES:

How to Boost Breakthrough Thinking by
Enlisting a Motley Crew

When people share similar perspectives, a group may be more susceptible to cognitive biases like the confirmation bias, which can lead them to pay attention to information confirming their shared point of view, while ignoring, or sometimes not even noticing, information that challenges it.[146] Groups with diverse ways of thinking, however, may consider more sources of information, explore more interpretations, and challenge each other's assumptions and biases.[147] People with distinctive perspectives tend to make unusual connections and look at problems differently, as well as the possible ways of solving problems. All of this can increase the possibility of breakthrough. But knowing the potential benefits of diversity is one thing; actually reaping those benefits on your own team can be something else entirely.

Enlisting a motley crew is about bringing together diverse perspectives, but also about creating the right conditions for team members to voice their unique points of view. It's about embracing both divergence and convergence—exploring various outlooks and uncovering what sets people apart, and then harnessing those differences for the good of the team. When you *enlist a motley crew*, your differences could transform from a potential threat to fuel for breakthrough.

The following are a set of powerful methods for helping teams and individuals effectively *enlist a motley crew*.

Enlist a Motley Crew Method 1: Reveal Your Superpower

Some of the characteristics that can influence one's perspectives on the world are visible—height is one example.
Many others, such as values, are hidden. Often people aren't aware of all the important aspects of their teammate's identities or why they might be important in the context of a particular situation. But you can tell them!

How to reveal your superpower:

Step 1: Collect images of various well-known celebrities, historical figures, superheroes, and/or other fictional characters.

Step 2: Ask each individual to choose one image that represents the unique perspective and/or superpower they'll bring to a meeting, project, or team.

Step 3: Go around the room and ask each person to share the image they selected and how they hope to apply their perspective and/or superpower to the task at hand.

Optional Step 4: Consider posting the images somewhere with the names of team members attached as a visual reminder of the diversity in the room.

NOTES:

Enlist a Motley Crew Method 2: Assess Your Team's Diversity

We ask in the *enlist a motley crew* chapter whether your teams are as diverse as Earnest Shackleton's crew, but of course there isn't a straightforward answer to that question—it depends on the lens you use. Shackleton's crew was quite diverse in terms of experiences and skills, and they had some level of age diversity, too, with a range of 20 to 48 years, but they had no gender diversity and only limited cultural diversity.[148] One might argue that it was the experience and skill diversity that mattered most in this case, but who knows what would have happened if Shackleton's grandmother had been along for the ride!

To assess your own teams' diversity, you may want to consider various layers to understand where you have diversity and where it's lacking. Or you might choose a particular lens, such as *Business Chemistry*, that by its nature represents different perspectives. Then consider how balanced the team is—does one group or perspective dominate the team? Are there groups or perspectives that are represented by either a single individual or just a few?

How to assess your team's diversity:

Step 1: Choose a lens or multiple lenses on which to assess diversity (e.g., *Business Chemistry* types, academic disciplines, gender, generations, or industries).

Step 2: Ask team members to indicate which group(s) they fall into.

Step 3: Illustrate your team's diversity with a series of pie charts or other visuals that represent the number of groups or perspectives represented, as well as the proportion of members in each group.

Step 4: Discuss how your team's diversity or lack thereof according to the chosen lens(es) might be supporting or harming your creative work together.

NOTES:

....

....

Enlist a Motley Crew Method 3: Mind the Gap

Suppose you've used *enlist a motley crew* method 2 of assessing your team's diversity and have discovered that your team is not very diverse. It's pretty common. Teams can become quite homogenous when particular functions attract or select a certain type of person with a shared perspective, such as a finance department hiring those who favor a concrete, quantitative approach. Lack of diversity can also result from teams and organizations selecting members based on cultural "fit" and adding new people who think a lot like those already there.[149]

If you feel your team isn't as motley as you'd like, it's particularly important for you to identify where you might have potential gaps. Assuming you're not able to immediately address those gaps by recruiting more team members, you may need other strategies to be mindful in the meantime.

How to mind the gap:

Step 1: Assess where your group may lack diversity using *enlist a motley crew* method 2.

Step 2: Identify where you may need to pay extra attention to represent a different perspective (e.g., maybe your team doesn't have any Guardians, so you'll need to make sure you're paying attention to details, potential risks, and underlying processes).

Step 3: Explore ways that your group could address these gap areas, for instance:

- Ask the group, or take turns individually, to adopt the style of the missing perspective in a discussion.

- Seek people from outside the group to represent the missing perspective in critical conversations.

- Implement processes to counteract some of the downsides of missing that perspective.

Step 4: Perform a group audit on a regular basis to see how well you're incorporating important missing perspectives.

NOTES:

Enlist a Motley Crew Method 4: Interrupt Cascades

Imagine trying to change the direction of a big waterfall. Without a feat of engineering, it would be impossible. That's how a *cascade* can work on a team: once ideas, discussion, and decision-making start flowing in a particular direction, momentum often keeps them moving that way.[150] Cascades can be particularly likely when a team's makeup is lopsided so that a particular perspective dominates. For example, a team of technical-focused people may go straight to discussing the technical aspects of a project without considering the interpersonal aspects. Or a team of risk-takers may move right to envisioning the possible downstream benefits of a direction, skipping right over the possible costs.

Even if diverse views exist on the team—maybe there are one or two people with a more interpersonal focus on that technical team or a few more prudent members on the team of risk-takers—they probably won't change the flow once it's established, because people often hesitate to voice disagreement with an idea that gets early visible support. Momentum can build for various reasons: *reputational* cascades can result from a fear of looking bad or of being punished for disagreeing, and *informational* cascades can occur when people assume that early speakers know something others don't. Either way, you can end up with self-censoring and groupthink, which means the team doesn't benefit from its diverse perspectives.

Because it can be very difficult to change the direction of a cascade once it starts, you'll want to interrupt a potential cascade before it gets going.

How to interrupt cascades:

Step 1: Start with assessing your team's diversity according to *enlist a motley crew* method 2 and identifying possible gaps where you might have a lighter representation of particular perspectives, as we suggest in *enlist a motley crew* method 3 (e.g., maybe you have mostly extroverts and few introverts, or maybe your team is made up of mostly people located in the United States with only a couple of people who reside in other countries).

Step 2: As you begin a team discussion, consider these techniques to interrupt a potential cascade:

- If you're the team leader, wait to share your perspective until later in the discussion, because a leader can have an outsized influence on the direction of a cascade.

- Acknowledge when particular perspectives may be likely to dominate and encourage anyone with a less common perspective to speak up early. This could give them a chance to influence the direction of the conversation before a cascade sets the course.

- Interrupt possible reputational cascades by expressing the value of contrary opinions—ask "who can articulate a contradictory perspective here?"

- Interrupt possible informational cascades by emphasizing the power of a beginner's mindset, as we discuss in the *strip away everything* chapter—ask for new, different ideas, rather than just repeats and support for what's already been said.

- Acknowledge and recognize those who are willing to offer different perspectives, contrary opinions, and new ideas.

NOTES:

Enlist a Motley Crew Method 5: Celebrate Slogans

Suppose you've got a big problem to solve and you approach it the way you typically solve problems—you're likely to get your typical solutions. But if you want breakthrough solutions, it could help to consider some new and different approaches. And as we discuss in the *make a mess* chapter, it might help even more if your team had some fun doing so. What could be more fun than slogans?

Consider what it would look like to approach your problem from the perspective of various slogans in the marketplace. For example, how might the same problem be tackled from the perspective of third-party slogans such as *just do it* versus *think different* versus *you're in good hands*? Then try out your own slogan-generating skills. What slogans could you come up with for various different perspectives, such as different industries, companies, organizational life stages, generations, or individual working styles. Even TV or movie characters can work to represent different perspectives. What would the slogans be for the characters on your favorite TV show? And what would it look like to approach your problem from the perspective of those different slogans?

How to celebrate slogans:

Step 1: Identify a lens you'd like to use (e.g., *Business Chemistry* types, generations, or TV characters).

Step 2: Create a slogan for each group or individual (e.g., for Pioneers, Guardians, Drivers, and Integrators, or for Gen Z, Millennials, Gen X, and Boomers).

As an example, slogans for the *Business Chemistry* types might look like this:

- Pioneers: YOLO.

- Guardians: It's all in the details.

- Integrators: Work with me, people!

- Drivers: It's not personal, it's business.

Step 3: Consider how you might apply each of your slogans to a problem you're trying to solve. How would it affect your approach? Which one could lead to the most creative solutions? The most feasible? The most risky? The most transformative?

Step 4: Outline and celebrate the strengths of each approach to drive home the power of *enlisting a motley crew*.

NOTES:

How to Boost
Breakthrough Thinking by
Getting Real

When interacting with colleagues, it can be easy to get caught up in the tasks that need to be completed, the problems that need to be solved, and the barriers that need to be overcome. You may not always be focused on your humanity—who you are, who your colleagues are, and what you and they really care about. And that can mean you're missing out on all kinds of benefits that can result when team environments support authenticity and vulnerability.

Getting real might mean that you share more about your core values, your aspirations and hopes for the future, your worries, disappointments, and failures. It might mean you talk more about your cultures, your histories, or your traditions. *Getting real* could mean revealing your personal challenges and triumphs too, your ideas big and small. It might mean you acknowledge and express your true opinions or your emotions. And when you *get real* together, it means you're encouraging others to do all of these things too. The result of sharing more is hiding less, and that means you can more fully take advantage of the perspectives on your team.

The following are a set of powerful methods for helping teams and individuals effectively *get real*.

Get Real Method 1: Start a Vulnerability Loop

When you take a risk and share something about your own life it can inspire someone else to do the same. This kind of authenticity can start a vulnerability loop, as we describe in the *get real* chapter. The vulnerability can lead to trust, which can lead to more vulnerability. If you're hoping to build trust with someone, you may want to start with getting vulnerable.

How to start a vulnerability loop:

Step 1: Reflect on your mistakes, insecurities, failures, or other vulnerabilities— what might you be willing to share with someone else?

Step 2: Share it. If it feels appropriate, explain why you're sharing (e.g., that you want to create an environment where vulnerability is encouraged or that you want to normalize failure as a necessary part of the path to breakthrough).

Step 3: If someone else shares a vulnerability in response to your sharing, thank them. If they share first, reciprocate with sharing a vulnerability of your own.

NOTES:

....

....

....

....

....

....

....

Get Real Method 2: Flag Highs and Lows

In order to get really real, you may first need to spend a bit of time figuring out who you are. The answer could take various forms, because there are many aspects that make up who you are, including your consciousness, personality, working style, identities, roles, and values. Here we'll focus on your values.

Your core values are your most deeply held beliefs about what's important in life. One way to identify your values would be to choose from a list. An alternative way is to consider the formative experiences in your life and examine how you felt about them—because those feelings are often a reflection of the values you hold dear.

For example, think of an experience that made you very angry. Now reflect on why you felt so angry in that situation. It's likely that one of your core values was trampled on. Did you feel disrespected perhaps? Was your sense of freedom threatened? Did you feel someone was being unkind? Whatever the source of your anger, it likely points to a value that's important to you. This method is built on the peaks and valleys exercise created by Professor Dave Logan.[151]

How to flag highs and lows:

Step 1: Draw a horizontal line representing the timeline of your life, from birth until now. At the point of your birth draw a vertical line.

Step 2: Think of the most formative 7 to 10 personal and professional experiences in your life. Chart them on the axis you've drawn. Use the horizontal line to indicate when each experience occurred and the vertical line to indicate how negative or positive it was for you.

Step 3: For each experience, ask yourself, "What values were honored or threatened that made it so positive or negative for me?" Jot these values down—there may be many for each experience.

Step 4: Consider your timeline and identify your top five values, taking into account which values appeared most often and which you feel most strongly about.

Step 5: Write a personal definition for each of your top five values—what does it mean for you, personally (e.g., you might write "honesty means to me that I always tell the truth, unless I believe it will cause great harm to someone else.")?

Optional Step 6: To get real with a colleague, pair up to share a few of your stories and/or values with each other. Identify whether you have any shared values and how they might relate to the work you do together.

Optional Step 7: To get real with your team, combine your group of two with another group of two and discuss any shared values you have identified *or* debrief as a full team, identify any common values, and discuss how they relate to the work you do together.

NOTES:

Get Real Method 3: Explore Trust

As we mention in the *get real* chapter, one of the reasons we recommend sharing more of and about your human self is because it can help build trust between people, which in turn can facilitate more engagement, creativity, and breakthrough thinking. And sharing your perspective *about* trust can be a very direct way to *get real* and create more trust at the same time.

You may be familiar with the concept of *love languages* popularized by author Gary Chapman in his book *The Five Love Languages*.[152] The concept is that people don't all have the same preferences for how to give or receive love. Trust can be similar in that people don't all have the same preferences for how to build trust or view indicators of trustworthiness in the same way. One person might interpret competence as a signal that someone is trustworthy and another might be looking for evidence of honesty. Talking about those preferences and differences can be a first step to understanding the best way to create trusting relationships with others.

How to explore trust:

Step 1: Fill in the blanks to answer the following questions:

- One thing you can always trust me to do is _____ .

- I know I can trust you when _____ .

- If you _____, you will lose my trust.

- The most important thing someone can do to gain my trust is _____ .

Step 2: Pair up with someone and discuss where your answers are similar or different.

NOTES:

....

....

Get Real Method 4: Ask Deeper Questions

Sometimes people want to *get real* but may be unsure whether others are interested in them personally, or how to go about offering up such information, or even whether it's appropriate in a professional setting. This may be particularly true of your more introverted colleagues. One of the best ways to encourage others to get real with you is to ask questions.

Although most everyone knows how to ask questions, doing so in a really impactful way is something different. In their 2018 *Harvard Business Review* article, "The Surprising Power of Questions," Harvard Business School professors Alison Wood Brooks and Leslie K. John encourage us to really work on our question-asking skills: "The good news is that by asking questions, we naturally improve our emotional intelligence, which in turn makes us better questioners—a virtuous cycle."[153] They suggest keeping questions open-ended, leaning into follow-up questions, and gradually building rapport by starting with less sensitive questions and then slowly escalating to build a closer bond. They also quote Dale Carnegie's 1936 classic *How to Win Friends & Influence People:* "Ask questions the other person will enjoy answering."[154] Sounds about right to us.

Authors Chris Colin and Rob Baedeker have some advice for encouraging people to get even more real with you.[155] They suggest asking for stories, not answers. So instead of "Where are you from?" try "What's the strangest thing about where you grew up?" Or instead of "What do you do?" try "How'd you end up in your line of work?" Or instead of "How are you?" try "What's different since we last met?" These questions can move you toward a deeper conversation, you could learn more about the other person, and they'll likely feel positively about their interaction with you.

How to ask deeper questions:

Step 1: Get curious. What do you want to know?

Step 2: Ask about it. Not sure where to start? Practice question storming, coming up with as many questions as you possibly can. Or let someone else come up with the questions—a quick internet search of "get to know you questions" will pull up thousands to choose from.

Step 3: Listen to the answer or story. (See *get real* method 5, next, for more on this one.)

Step 4: Pay attention to the person's comfort level with sharing so that you don't push too far too fast. Do they seem hesitant or eager to share? Calibrate the next step based on that assessment.

Step 5: Ask some more. If you find it difficult to think of great follow-up questions on the spot, start with these basics:

- Would you say more about that?

- Would you give me an example of that?

- What did you think/feel about that?

- Would you tell me more about why you think that's important/interesting?

- What do you think should happen next?"

NOTES:

Get Real Method 5: Listen

If someone is getting real with you, you'll want to listen up! This is especially important if you've just asked them a question. ☺ Just how important is it to listen? We asked more than 25,000 professionals, "What is the *one* thing someone can do to build trust with you?" And the most common answer by far was "*listen*."[156] Hundreds of our survey respondents didn't say anything more; they just wrote the one word. What could be more simple? And we'd bet you're doing it already, but what does it mean to *really* listen?

For one thing, if you want someone to really feel listened to, you'll need to stop doing all those other things you're trying to do at the same time. If you tend to secretly multitask while on Zoom calls, guess what? It's probably not a secret. People can likely tell that you're multitasking. Or are you sleeping? (That's what it looks like when you're looking down at your phone.) Neither one is great for trust building. And if you're together in person, they can tell *for sure* when you're multitasking. Whether online or in person, failing to focus means you could be missing an important opportunity to build trust and encourage people to *get real*.

Another way to let people know you're listening is through your body language, such as when you make eye contact, nod, or smile. Not only do these behaviors demonstrate that you're listening, research also suggests that eye contact and smiling can promote trust.[157] If you're talking with someone on video, smiling and nodding may be particularly important, because eye contact can be a bit tricky; it looks like you're making eye contact if you look at the camera versus the screen, but then you can't *actually* look at the other person's image. Of course, if you're talking on the phone without video, none of these cues will be visible, so you'll have to indicate you're listening in other ways, like an occasional "uh-huh," "go on," or "I see."

When someone's *getting real* with you, it can be tempting to interrupt to tell them how much you relate to their experience and then to share a story about how a similar thing happened to you. Resist this urge. Likewise, it's important to listen to understand someone rather than to be ready to add your thoughts next. If your mind is focused on how to respond, it's difficult to process what your ears are hearing. And jumping in too fast with a response may make the other person feel you didn't really listen to everything they said.

How to listen:

Step 1: Focus on the person who is speaking without doing anything else.

Step 2: Show that you're listening through your body language or verbal cues.

Step 3: When the person is done speaking, acknowledge or reiterate what has been said.

Step 4: Ask follow-up questions.

NOTES:

How to Boost Breakthrough Thinking by
Making a Mess

Just like the age-old adage that you can't make omelets without breaking a few eggs, so too you can't tap into your full breakthrough potential if you want things to be neat, tidy, and predictable from start to finish. Breakthrough is rarely a linear process; it's only in hindsight and reflective narrative that it might look cleaner. Breakthrough is messy, but the point is not to stop at the mess but to embrace the mess as a way of getting to something better. There is a spectrum between having an idea and bringing it fully to life; the part in between is called the "messy middle" for a reason.

Make a mess is about practical experimentation. It's about being forced to not just articulate but to implement your assumptions and try them on for size. To cocreate and iterate, and get people engaged. *Make a mess* is not just about getting to a better final solution but about better understanding the problem and shedding light on new paths to solutions.

The following are a set of powerful methods for helping teams and individuals effectively *make a mess*.

Make a Mess Method 1: Go Marshmallow!

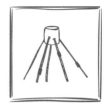

Tom Wujec's "Spaghetti Marshmallow Challenge," which we relay in the *make a mess* chapter, has spread through seminars and science classes to 1,000s of prototyping groups worldwide.[158] One of the key takeaways from analyzing these numerous spaghetti tower challenges is that kids often outperform executives. Although adults spend most of their time concocting a plan and determining who's in charge, kids prototype and play with the materials from the beginning. Each time a last-minute marshmallow placement causes another "perfectly planned" tower to collapse with no time left to redesign, the prototype-from-the-get-go kids could notch another tally in the win column.

Trying this challenge yourself is a fun way to get creative juices flowing for your own team to prime the pumps for breakthrough and to demonstrate the power of *making a mess*.

How to go marshmallow:

Step 1: Divide your group into teams of four and give them the following supplies:

- 20 sticks of spaghetti

- 1 yard of string

- 1 yard of masking tape

- 1 standard-sized marshmallow

- 1 stopwatch or time-keeping device

Be sure to place all these items in a paper bag on the team's table to hide the ingredients and maximize the "surprise and delight."

Step 2: Explain the challenge and guidelines:

Challenge:

- Build the tallest freestanding structure: The winning team is the one that has the tallest structure measured from the surface of the tabletop to the top of the marshmallow. This means the structure cannot be suspended from a higher structure such as a chair, ceiling, or chandelier.

Guidelines:

- The entire marshmallow must be on top of the structure: Cutting, tearing, or eating your mallow to lighten the load disqualifies the team.

- Use as much or as little of the kit as desired. Teams may also break up all materials except the marshmallow.

- Teams have 18 minutes to complete the challenge. If possible, display a large countdown timer to *dial up the drama*.

- Any team touching or holding the structure after the time runs out, should be disqualified.

Step 3: When the time is up, measure the still-standing towers, declare a winner, and debrief with the teams on key lessons they can take away from the challenge.

NOTES:

....

....

....

....

....

....

Make a Mess Method 2: Make a Metaphor

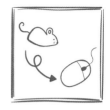

Innovation is often fueled by metaphor or analogous examples. Henry Ford famously was inspired to develop the production line after touring meat-packing houses.[159] George de Mestral got the idea for Velcro from burrs sticking to his pants after a hike.[160] With this method, we're suggesting you don't just wait for inspiration to come to you (though be open to it when it does!), but instead create a metaphor that helps push thinking and that people can relate to intuitively, without necessarily knowing all the details.

Say, for example, that you're trying to find a way to streamline the registration process for a professional certification exam. Currently, people find the process laborious, tedious, and burdensome. Maybe you think of the metaphor of skiing and how easy it is to just shush down the slopes when there's a new covering of powder. What if the process could feel that easy? As you play with this idea more, you realize that the speed of skiing makes it potentially a bit scary, but also exhilarating and fun. Connecting back to the process for exam registration, you think about how nervous people might feel just before their exam, and how you could balance that by creating an experience that is not only easy but maybe even fun. By continuing to play with a metaphor for something that is well known, such as skiing, you can better tease out aspects of your challenge. This can help inspire new associations and insights about the idea, as well as reveal potential requirements and assumptions to be further tested. As Steven Pinker shares in *The Stuff of Thought*, "The power of analogy doesn't come from noticing a mere similarity of parts. . . . It comes from noticing relations among parts, even if the parts themselves are very different."[161] This process becomes even more powerful if you physically represent the metaphors in some way, even if the physical model is imperfect.

How to make a metaphor:

Step 1: Think through your challenge and identify the general problem you're looking to solve. For instance, for Velcro, the general problem was how to stick something to something else but still be able to remove it without too much hassle. With the professional certification exam registration example, it was getting someone through a journey with speed and ease. Come up with a list of things that characterize your situation.

Step 2: Once you have that list, consider what other things also address that problem or need, or have those characteristics. For instance, if your idea is about how to tailor something to the context or environment, think of other things that do that, for example, chameleons, concierge doctors, and so on. Choose one that best evokes the foundational concepts of your idea.

Step 3: Bring your metaphor to life by sketching it out as a drawing, or putting it together with Legos, or collage pictures from magazines. Push yourself to actually create something physical and visual, highlighting key characteristics that illustrate various facets of the metaphor.

Step 4: Make connections between the metaphor and your idea. Think about other potential correlations. For example, just like skiers can go faster with better equipment, people can register for exams more quickly with faster internet. Consider what assumptions you're making that lead to correlations. For example, maybe you assume skiers and exam registrants need to use their own equipment. Highlight where there are inconsistencies between your idea and the metaphor as well, and consider potential implications of these differences. For instance, skiers will take a run multiple times, whereas exam takers would ideally only do a full registration once.

Step 5: If you do this exercise with a group, share each person's individual metaphors and visual representations with the group and identify common patterns in terms of themes, characteristics, and assumptions.

NOTES:

Make a Mess Method 3: Immerse Yourself

There's a saying in real estate that it's all about location, location, location. Turns out that's important for breakthrough as well. When we say location, in this case we don't necessarily mean a specific place, but rather the environment in which you locate yourself. Research has shown that environments can influence everything from mood to stress levels, enhance memory and learning, and promote cognitive flexibility.[162]

In our Deloitte Greenhouses, we construct immersive environments to activate people not only intellectually but also emotionally and physically through visceral, evocative experiences. Our methodology builds on many disciplines including an interesting concept in psychology called embodied cognition, which posits that the body, and the body's movements and experiences, can influence the mind.[163] This generally results in significantly deeper engagement, greater trust and openness, and increased diversity of ideas.

Through thousands of these immersive sessions, we've found there is power in surrounding people with activating visuals and artifacts. Moreover, a less perfect immersion, particularly one cocreated by the participants, is particularly conducive to breakthrough thinking. Our experience is consistent with research that suggests that less orderly environments produce greater creativity.[164]

How to immerse yourself:

Step 1: Determine what context best makes sense for your problem or initial idea. Are you in a hospital? A home? Another planet?

Step 2: Provide your group with materials to construct their environment(s). Include blank canvas kind of materials such as posters, whiteboards, and so on, as well as evocative props such as furniture, paintings, stuffed animals, fake campfires . . . whatever might be helpful in setting the scene. Don't worry about being too precise—part of what makes the process messy is having things that don't quite fit that people find a way to work in.

Step 3: Use the materials to create a physical landscape, ideally one that surrounds you and the team so you feel like you are within that environment versus on the side observing it. Encourage everyone to contribute to the building effort in parallel. Resist the temptation to assign an architect or chief builder. Remember, a bit of chaos here is good.

Step 4: Once your environment(s) are complete, spend time within the environment discussing your idea. (For example, talk about how customers might order a product at a fully automated store while inside the mock-up you've built of that store.) Play out different scenarios within the space.

Step 5: Keep iterating on your environment as needed to reflect the discussions!

NOTES:

Make a Mess Method 4: Stream Your Consciousness

Humans can be their own worst judges, particularly when trying to come up with brilliant, breakthrough ideas (we warn you about that internal cynic in the *silence your cynic* chapter). *Is that really a genius concept or is it stupid? I don't think this is the best way to describe this—maybe I should wordsmith it a bit more?*

Rather than stall yourself out on a quest for perfection, instead embrace the opposite and just get the ideas out of your head as quickly as possible. No editing. This is an approach to personal brainstorming that lets you capture a lot of raw material that you can then sort through and polish to your heart's content. If you want to do this with a group, simply have each individual complete the process and then compare your end results.

How to stream your consciousness:

Step 1: Open up a notes or document program on your computer and create a fresh document. (Note: This can be done on paper as well, but digital capture can sometimes be more effective.)

Step 2: Turn the brightness level down so that it's hard to see what you're writing.

Step 3: Set a timer for 10 minutes. It can help to play music during this time.

Step 4: Start typing by describing your challenge, for example, "I'm trying to figure out a new way to help schools prevent bullying."

Step 5: Keep on writing, just typing whatever it is that comes into your head. Don't worry if it isn't well written, or if you're jumping from one point to another without bridging sentences, or if you're misspelling words. The intent is to let your mind wander around this topic while you capture its journey.

Step 6: Continue writing until the timer is up. It may feel like a long time, but just stick with it. If ideas come less quickly toward the end (like the way popcorn kernels slow down their popping near the end of their microwave cycle) that's okay . . . some will still pop.

Step 7: After the timer ends, turn the brightness back up and look back at what you've written. Now you can allow your more logical brain to take back over and evaluate the mess. Are there some interesting themes to explore further? Some side points that might merit consideration? Different ways of potentially talking about the challenge with others? If you're doing this with a group, try to compare and contrast across the individual messes.

NOTES:

Make a Mess Method 5: Draw It Out

Have you ever been in a meeting and suddenly you notice that you've covered your notebook in doodles? Or maybe you're more conscious of your scribbling habits, thoughtfully embellishing margins with swoops and flourishes till nary an open space can be seen? Either way, we approve!

Much has been written about the potential health benefits of doodling, from decreasing stress to increasing focus. But when it comes to breakthrough, we're particular fans of its role in enhancing creativity. Doodling can help kick your brain into gear to get you into the flow and overcome the inertia of staring at a blank page.[165]

And remember, a doodle is defined as a rough drawing scribbled absentmindedly, so don't worry if you're not an artist. The process and flow are what's important versus a polished product, so go ahead and embrace your doodley mess!

How to draw it out:

Step 1: Write your challenge or opportunity in a single word or sentence in the middle of a blank page.

Step 2: Set a timer for three minutes. Bonus points for putting on a song from your Breakthrough Mix in the background (see *dial up the drama* method 4).

Step 3: Let your mind wander, pick up a pen, and begin doodling.

Step 4: When the time is up, pin your doodle up somewhere you can see it or keep it nearby to add to your doodle throughout the day.

NOTES:

How to Boost Breakthrough Thinking by Not Playing "Nice"

Working on teams means, by definition, that you're working with others. And although it might be something most people do on a regular basis, that doesn't mean everyone is an expert at it. Team environments, dynamics, and working norms, as well as individual styles, can all influence how people work together and whether they're supporting or undermining breakthrough thinking. Some people may seem too brash and others too timid. Some might be perceived as pushing too hard and others appear too passive. Some might be experienced as too harsh and others too gentle. *Not playing "nice"* is about finding a middle ground. It's about giving honest feedback, with caring, about voicing disagreement respectfully, and about pointing out elephants then taming them together. Ultimately, *not playing "nice"* is about creating the right environment for powerful relationships that not only allow but also explicitly encourage the kind of honest interactions needed for breakthrough.

The following are a set of powerful methods for helping teams and individuals effectively *not play "nice."*

Don't Play "Nice"
Method 1: Save a Seat for the
Elephant

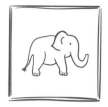

Author Timothy Clark characterizes *intellectual bravery* as "a willingness to disagree, dissent, or challenge the status quo in a setting of social risk in which you could be embarrassed, marginalized, or punished in some way." In a 2020 *Harvard Business Review* article, he suggests that "when intellectual bravery disappears, organizations develop patterns of willful blindness. Bureaucracy buries boldness. Efficiency crushes creativity. From there, the status quo calcifies and stagnation sets in."[166] That doesn't sound very good if what you're looking for is breakthrough.

Cultivating a culture of intellectual bravery can be serious business, but sometimes adding a light-hearted twist can make it easier to do. One of our favorite ways to keep the *don't play "nice"* principle top of mind in our Deloitte Greenhouse spaces is to reserve a seat for a big stuffed elephant. When someone wants to call out an uncomfortable truth, they can hold up the elephant or toss it across the room. One of the great things about our plush elephant is it allows people to point something out in a way that feels friendly and a little bit playful. If a session is virtual, we sometimes feature an elephant in a different place on each slide, and we encourage participants to annotate directly on the screen when they feel there's something that needs to be acknowledged.

How to save a seat for the elephant:

Step 1: Bring a big stuffed elephant into the room and give it a seat at the table.

Step 2: Invite people to hold up, toss, or refer to the elephant when they feel a potentially uncomfortable point needs to be made.

NOTES:

Don't Play "Nice"
Method 2: Go to Extremes

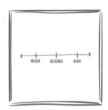

Speaking a truth in harsh tones may make a problem very apparent, but it can also create an environment that feels hostile and lacks a sense of safety. It's like directly pointing at someone—clear, but rude. However, similar to nodding in someone's direction rather than pointing, being too timid or indirect may confuse people or cause them to look right past the problem you're trying to call attention to. It's likely that somewhere in the middle of those two extremes is where you'll want your message to fall if you're hoping for breakthrough on your team.

To call out a truth or deliver a potentially uncomfortable message in a way that supports breakthrough isn't something everyone is naturally skilled at. But practice makes progress, and it's likely that the more you work at finding the right words and the right tone, the better you'll get. Instead of just winging it, it can be easier to get things right after spending some focused time thinking about, and even writing down, the words that could best convey the message in the most appropriate tone.

How to go to extremes:

Step 1: Identify a truth that needs pointing out or a potentially uncomfortable message that needs delivering.

Step 2: Draw a horizontal line with the labels "Too Weak" on the far left and "Too Blunt" on the far right.

Step 3: Ask yourself (or the team), "What's the most direct, potentially offensive, way we could communicate this message?" Write the answers on the far right side of the line.

Step 4: Then ask, "What's the wimpiest way we could communicate this message?" Write the answers on the far left side of the line.

Step 5: Consider and/or discuss where on the line between these two extremes is appropriate for this situation. Think about how to raise the issue, when to raise it, what method will be used for communicating the message, what environment it will be delivered in, and exactly what to say.

Step 6: Consider how the *Business Chemistry* of the message recipient might affect all of the aforementioned (e.g., Drivers like directness and Integrators prefer more diplomacy).

NOTES:

Don't Play "Nice"
Method 3: Find Your
Achilles Heel

Have you ever said "just playing devil's advocate" to make a criticism feel more palatable? People tend to do so because it enables them to distance themselves from a critical message and makes it easier to go against the grain. When done well—to present a contrary opinion or alternative idea, rather than to attack a person—it can be an effective technique to boost your critical thinking, improve your decision-making, and make your ideas better.

Sometimes people can be more honest about criticisms if there's explicit permission to do so or a structure that allows them to distance themselves from the criticism. If you want to discourage people from *playing "nice"* in regard to an idea your team is working on, no need to involve the devil: ask them to play the role of your most likely critics. Doing so can give people permission to surface criticisms they might otherwise hesitate to share.

How to find your Achilles heel:

Step 1: Identify the likely worst critics of your idea (e.g., analyst community, board of directors, your boss, your employees, the press, your competitors).

Step 2: Choose one likely critic and look at your idea from their perspective. Expose the weaknesses in the idea by outlining their likely criticisms. What "gotcha" questions might that critic ask that you wish you'd researched? What would they say to negate your argument?

Step 3: Choose another critic and repeat step 2. Then do it again until you've worked through all the likely critics.

Step 4: Consider themes in the critiques—are any of them shared across critics?

Step 5: Identify ways to overcome the obstacles you've identified. Discuss patterns and themes that emerged, any assumptions that were revealed, and implications.

Don't Play "Nice"
Method 4: Like, Wish, and Wonder

Using a positive tone can make feedback easier to deliver and more palatable to accept. It can also increase psychological safety in a group. Aiming for a positive tone isn't about *playing "nice"*; it's about sharing constructive feedback in a way that feels supportive. Providing people with some structure can make it easier to strike the right tone, especially when that structure asks everyone to offer praise and constructive criticism. The method described here has been popularized by Stanford Design School.[167]

How to like, wish, and wonder:

Step 1: When someone shares an idea, start with what you like about it. For example, "I like how creative and bold this idea is."

Step 2: Then follow up with what you'd suggest changing or would like to see more or less of. For example, "I wish we had a clearer idea about how it could work within the context of these very real barriers we're facing."

Step 3: Then build on the idea or make a suggestion. For example, "I wonder if we might pressure test the idea against those barriers one by one."

NOTES:

Don't Play "Nice"
Method 5: Frame Feedback

Often, it's empathy that prevents people from giving and getting feedback. One study suggests that leaders with more empathy feel worse after giving critical feedback than those with less empathy.[168] Our own research has also shown that Integrators, the *Business Chemistry* type with the most empathy, are most likely to say they'd be discouraged from sharing if they thought it might make someone else feel criticized.[169]

If you're holding back feedback that could benefit someone else, try looking at things through their lens to help you see why you may actually be doing them a favor by sharing. Then deliver the feedback with care.

If you want feedback from someone else and you're not getting it, you could try to see things from their perspective to understand why they're not offering it. Then make it easier on them (and potentially more helpful for you) by asking for advice rather than feedback. Although giving feedback on someone's past behavior can feel critical, giving advice about what to do in the future feels less so. One program of research at Harvard Business School found that when people asked for advice instead of feedback they got input that was more helpful for their development—it was more actionable and future focused.[170]

How to frame feedback:

Step 1: Spend a moment thinking about the other person as a human, someone with hopes, dreams, fears, and insecurities. Consider why you want to help them grow or why you want them, in particular, to help you.

Step 2a: If you've got input that you're hesitating to provide, make a list of ways in which sharing it will benefit the other person. This list is just for you.

Step 2b: If you'd like input from someone who seems hesitant to provide it, make a list of ways in which their sharing it will benefit you. Include these reasons in your request for input.

Step 3a: To share your input with someone else, frame it as advice. Express why you want to help them grow.

Step 3b: To request input from someone else, ask for advice. Express why you want them, in particular, to help you.

NOTES:

How to Boost
Breakthrough Thinking by
Dialing Up the Drama

Drama is . . . drumroll please . . . a mighty but often underused force for breakthrough. It grabs people's attention and engages their focus. It can tap into their emotions, activating them more fully as human beings. And it gets the brain going in a way that can be conducive to imagination, originality, and divergent ideation.

Dialing up the drama is also important even once you've found that breakthrough, as a means to make the aha more compelling and less threatening for others. It can make an idea more memorable and contagious, increasing the likelihood that the breakthrough actually comes to fruition.

There are many ways to *dial up the drama*, from activating individual senses to sensory immersion to using comedy. To promote breakthrough, individual dramatic factors can be treated as unique ingredients that you bring together in varying amounts and combinations. There's no set recipe, so experiment with mixing and matching these elements to whet your, and others', breakthrough palates. Bon appetit!

The following are a set of powerful methods for helping teams and individuals effectively *dial up the drama.*

Dial Up the Drama
Method 1: Kick It Around

Physically acting out an idea is a powerful way to engage people while also stimulating their brain in different ways. This is the concept of embodied cognition that we mention in the *make a mess* chapter.[171] Furthermore, research shows that people are faster at responding to metaphoric phrases having performed a relevant body movement than when they did not move at all.[172] In this case, we are exploring the metaphor of "kicking" around an idea.

How to kick it around:

Step 1: Take a sticky note and write down one key word that summarizes the subject of the brainstorming session. Then, take a ball and attach the sticky note to the ball.

Step 2: Ask participants to stand up and organize themselves in a circle. Explain that the point of the exercise is to generate thoughts about the identified subject of the brainstorming session by literally "kicking around the idea." Identify someone to play the role of note taker.

Step 3: Explain that the ball will be kicked to a participant to start the brainstorm. When the ball comes to an individual, they should briefly share an idea on the subject and then kick the ball to someone else. Capture ideas on a separate board/chart.

Step 4: Continue until everyone in the group has kicked the ball and shared an idea.

Step 5: Consider playing music to increase energy during the exercise.

Step 6: Facilitate a discussion to refine the ideas that were generated.

NOTES:

Dial Up the Drama
Method 2: Color Me
Breakthrough

What you see can dramatically affect your emotions and processing, whether what you're seeing is your environment (images, structures, and setting around you), particular content that's being shared or is otherwise visible (presentations, charts, etc.), or characteristics of the people who are present (body language, power dynamics, etc.). One of the notable aspects of sight is color. There is a body of study known as color psychology that explores the connection between perception of color and human behavior. How color affects people may differ based on culture, gender, age, or personal experience; however, research suggests that some effects are more universal. In particular, the colors green, blue, and yellow have been associated with more creative thinking.[173] What's not inspiring? The colors white and gray, which are unfortunately often the palette choice for office spaces and other business environments. Here's how to use color to support breakthrough thinking.

How to color me breakthrough:

Step 1: Take note of your surroundings—what's the color vibe?

Step 2: If the space you're in isn't colored for breakthrough, either move to an environment that has green, blue, and perhaps yellow (bonus points for places with natural light and green plants), *or* do what you can to decorate your space with these colors. Posters, throw pillows, and portable plants are a great temporary fix. If you have the ability, go a step further and actually paint a wall in one of these colors.

Step 3: Mix it up. There can be cultural and personal associations with colors, so try different options to find your breakthrough groove.

NOTES:

Dial Up the Drama
Method 3: Light It Up

Light is a powerful tool for breakthrough thinking. Natural light in particular can provide a strong creative boost, according to Human Spaces research which showed a 15% improvement in creativity correlated with exposure to natural light.[174]

Light can also be used for dramatic effect. In one Deloitte Greenhouse session, we had participants exploring future scenarios. The room was dark, illuminated only in targeted work zones filled with colored LEDs, digital displays, and animated projections. After working for a while in this focused manner, participants were told we were about to bring their ideas to life. As we made this announcement, we raised the blackout blinds on all the windows, flooding the space with natural light and expansive views. The effect was striking and instantly sparked heightened energy and conversation, while metaphorically symbolizing the dawn of emerging opportunities.

How to light it up:

Step 1: Find an environment where you can control the light levels (e.g., probably not outside).

Step 2: Determine the effect you are trying to get—are you going from dark to light, such as in our example? Are you trying to put a spotlight on a particular area? Do you want to use different light colors in order to emphasize a theme?

Step 3: Create and implement a lighting plan designed to elicit the kind of effect you're going for. If you're with a group, be sure to assign a producer to manage the lights, and provide clear cues so they know what to do, when.

NOTES:

Dial Up the Drama
Method 4: Make a Playlist

Many people have phones filled with playlists, chosen to suit their activities or moods. Some may even still have a mix tape or two lying around from pre-streaming days where road trips were fueled in part by thoughtfully curated and hand recorded musical selections. Well now's your opportunity to add a new option to your repertoire: your Breakthrough Mix.

Music is a powerful activator to influence moods, enhance and evoke memories, and stimulate creativity by increasing divergent thinking. Indeed, a recent study showed that listening to happy classical music in particular led to more innovative solutions, regardless of whether or not people actually liked the music.[175]

To set the right tone for breakthrough, try to find music that's not only "happy" but that also relates to your issue or opportunity in some way to provide additional layers of relevant drama.

How to make a playlist:

Step 1: Think about your issue or opportunity—is there a theme that somehow relates? For instance, if you're considering opportunities to expand into new markets, you might think about a theme of *exploration* or *adventure*. If you're looking to improve efficiency you might choose a theme of *speed*.

Step 2: Search your favorite music providers for songs matching your theme (internet searches can help) that are upbeat in nature.

Step 3: Sequence the songs into a playlist. For extra dramatic effect, follow an arc in which the first song sets the theme and the tone, the subsequent songs build on it, and the final song brings it home.

Step 4: Share your playlist as appropriate, and encourage others to add their favorites as well!

Step 5: Rock on.

Dial Up the Drama
Method 5: Be a Character

Breakthrough can be elusive, like a mythical creature whose movements you can sense at the edge of your vision but can't quite capture in your lens. To bring it into better focus, it can help to stop looking from a distance and instead observe things from a more intimate vantage point by putting yourself in a different context. One way to do this is to cast yourself as a character directly affected by the challenge that you're trying to solve in order to stimulate deeper empathy and ideation. So for instance, instead of thinking theoretically about what might help people caring for aging parents, you would imagine yourself as a person caring for a parent, or potentially as the aging parent even, and then further explore the opportunity within that role.

How to be a character:

Step 1: Think about the issue you're trying to solve as if it were the plot of a movie. Think about the main characters who would be part of that storyline, for instance, a caretaker, a parent, a concerned citizen, a health care provider, and so on.

Step 2: Divide the group into breakout groups and have each group choose a character to develop together, or, if you're working individually, choose a character for yourself.

Step 3: Give each group a large poster and ask them to develop their character's story. Who are they? What is their name? What do they do? What do they like?

Step 4: After the background is created, think about some of the key moments where that character is affected by, or themselves affect, the topic at hand. For instance, an elderly parent falling and needing to get help. These are "moments of truth" for the characters involved.

Step 5: Consider a series of questions relative to each moment of truth:

- How is this moment of truth affecting your character? How do they feel? What do they need? What do they wish for?

- What other characters are engaged in this moment and how?

- How might we adjust the scenario to better suit the character?

Step 6: Have each character share their perspective with the broader group. Encourage them to speak in the first person as if they are the character when they are speaking. Bonus points for adding costumes and other props as a way to reinforce the identification with the character.

NOTES:

How to Boost
Breakthrough Thinking by
Making Change

There's a familiar saying that the only constant is change. Although this is true for life in general, we've found that actively *making change* sometimes requires intentional practice. First, to identify your own degree of openness and approach to change. Next, to persevere through the iterative process of making change, explore possible diverging pathways, and perhaps even push oneself past beloved ideas. And finally, to focus on making a change that is meaningful, drawing on one's own and others' resources to scale impact.

The following are a set of powerful methods for helping teams and individuals effectively *make change*.

Make Change Method 1: Navel Gaze

Your working style can have a big impact on how you make change, but chances are you may not be aware of it. *Business Chemistry* is one useful lens for helping understand how the way you think, process information, and engage might present challenges and opportunities when it comes to getting to breakthrough. Even without an assessment or a structured system, you can glean a lot about yourself through some guided introspection.

How to navel gaze:

Step 1: Consider your preferences and behaviors from several different angles:

- Are you comfortable with risk or do you try to minimize it?

- Are you a quick decision-maker or a more deliberate one?

- Do you make decisions based more on data or intuition?

- How much advance thought do you put into potential implications?

- How important do you feel it is to reach consensus?

Step 2: Think about how your answers to these questions might affect how you make change?

- Are you likely to resist change or promote it?

- What emotions are likely to come up for you in the face of change?

- Are you likely to tire of iterations or dig in to continue to adapt your ideas?

- What's your approach for rallying support and resources and how will that affect your ability to drive change?

- Do you tend to push or pull others toward change?

Step 3: Make a plan. Think about what kind of change will be needed for your breakthrough idea and develop a strategy for how to bring the best of yourself to that change and to shore up areas where you are likely to be more challenged. Be ready to rinse and repeat—keep assessing and evolving as you move to realize your idea!

NOTES:

_____

_____

_____

_____

_____

_____

_____

_____

_____

_____

_____

_____

_____

_____

Make Change Method 2: Establish Rituals

Rituals can be found throughout human history and across cultures. They are patterns of actions done repeatedly that elevate a moment and give it meaning, and they can be powerful tools to help individuals and groups process and manage significant change. As Margaret Hagan and Kursat Ozenc share in their book *Rituals for Work*, rituals can help decrease anxiety, increase feelings of control, and increase creativity among other positive benefits.[176]

Although there are many possible moments in which to use rituals to enhance performance and stimulate breakthrough, three are particularly important for *making change*:

• When something fails and you need to shift directions

• When you choose to self-disrupt

• When you have an aha that propels you forward

In the Deloitte Greenhouse we once worked with a team that had spent months working on a product idea only to determine that it ultimately wasn't viable as conceived and needed significant revision. Rather than sweeping the perceived "failure" under the rug, the executive team decided to bring in a band for a surprise New Orleans style "funeral march." They used the ritual to honor the work of the team and celebrate that they had discovered some critical insights that would be essential for future success. They've since adapted this ritual to a more portable version (full jazz bands were hard to cram into the office) to celebrate failures as essential milestones in the process of getting to breakthrough.

Note that rituals are in some ways an expression of a culture, so thought should be taken as to how best to match the group's need with the specific ritual, and provide room for the participants to further shape it to make it their own.

How to establish rituals:

Step 1: Think about the three types of *making change* moments and what they may look like for your group. Determine:

- *How* will you know the moment is happening?

- *What* would you like to have happen as a result of the ritual relative to that moment? For instance, with our prior example, if something fails, the intent was to raise visibility and celebrate the discovery of a way that didn't work.

Step 2: Design a ritual for each moment, considering:

- *Where* and *when* would you have the ritual relative to this moment?

- *Who* would be involved in this ritual?

- *What* would be the main activities in your ritual, with a clear flow from start to finish?

- *How* might you enhance the symbolism and meaning of your ritual with props (a physical award) or actions (a movement or gesture)?

Step 3: Socialize your ritual ideas with others and let them help shape and refine them to best suit the culture.

Step 4: Try out your rituals and in true *make change* fashion, continue to adapt and evolve!

NOTES:

Make Change Method 3: Motivate with Nudges

Popularized by Richard Thaler and Cass Sunstein in their book *Nudge*, nudges are small changes in the environment that are easy and inexpensive to implement and can help significantly change human behavior.[177] For example, organizations sometimes encourage people to take advantage of their 401K programs by making it the default choice—employees have to actively indicate they do *not* want to participate if that's the case. The idea is to make it more likely that an individual will make a particular choice, or behave in a particular way, by altering the environment so that automatic cognitive processes are triggered to favor the desired outcome.

Nudge theory has been used across the public and private sectors. At Holborn Station, for example, Transport for London found that it was actually more efficient to have passengers stand on both sides of the escalators, rather than the common practice of "walk on the left, stand on the right." In order to make passengers comply, a combination of "standard" and "light" messages were developed with the help of the behavioral science department at the London School of Economics. Some of the cues included a talking projection of a staff member, an electronic version of the triangular "stand on the right" signs, signs on the floors, footprints on the escalator steps, handprints on the handrails, and station announcements. Studies show that this method increased capacity on the escalators by 30%.[178]

In Japan a number of mechanisms are deployed to nudge behavior in its train system. For example, instead of a harsh buzzer to signal a train's imminent departure, the major rail operator JR East commissioned Yamaha and composer Hiroaki Ide to create hassha melodies—short, ear-pleasing jingles that notify commuters of a train's imminent departure without inducing anxiety. A study conducted in October 2008 at Tokyo Station, for instance, found a 25% reduction in the number of passenger injuries attributable to rushing after the introduction of hassha melodies on certain platforms.[179]

How to motivate with nudges:

Step 1: Consider the change you are trying to make and whose behaviors will need to adjust in order for that change to take hold.

Step 2: Create a motivational map for each key group or category of individuals (e.g., daily commuters) by building out the following:

- What are their hopes and fears?

- What incentives appeal to them?

- What are current barriers to adoption?

- What things are likely to influence them?

Step 3: Consider where you might be able to create specific nudges to tilt individuals in the direction of change you desire:

- What could be changed in the environment?

- What could be changed in the positioning of the choice—how it's phrased or where it's communicated?

- What could be changed in the process itself?

Step 4: Look for opportunities to pilot your hypothesis (maybe *make a mess* a little) to learn and iterate on your plan.

NOTES:

Make Change Method 4: Plan for Scenarios

In order to evolve your ideas and continue to *make change*, it can help to develop and think through multiple potential futures in advance. Doing so may enable you to be more agile in responding to unforeseen circumstances, shape context as more information emerges, and adapt your idea to ensure sustainable impact.

How to plan for scenarios:

Step 1: Identify driving forces—what is happening in the world around you that might affect your breakthrough idea coming to fruition:

- Society

- Economics

- Politics

- Technology

Step 2: Select two of those forces to consider as the major uncertainties to evaluate.

Step 3: Use the two uncertainties to create a 2×2, with each uncertainty on an axis. So, for instance, if one uncertainty is *recession* and the other uncertainty is *willingness to travel*, we could create the following 2×2 with four associated scenarios:

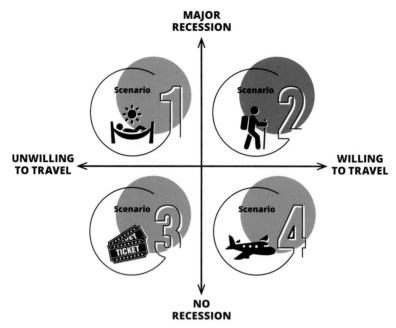

Copyright © 2023 Deloitte Development LLC. All rights reserved.

Step 4: Discuss the implications and impact of each scenario and consider how that might affect your approach.

NOTES:

Make Change Method 5: Find Your Why

Making significant change, and having people buy into that change, often require deep understanding and buy-in to the why. Simon Sinek, inspirational speaker and author of the book *The Power of Why*, developed the concept of the golden circle based on this insight as a result of studying what sets great organizations apart from others.[180] Just talking about *what* you plan to do, and *how* you plan to do it, may not be sufficient to motivate people to make big change; the *why* is what inspires action. It could provide a cause that can transcend a goal.

In our Deloitte Greenhouse experiences, we've found it can be helpful to think about the *why* for change at three levels:

- Why are the changes important to the organization (or to society as a whole)?

- Why are the changes important to the team (or to customers or another stakeholder group)?

- Why are the changes important to you personally?

Organizational *whys* might include responses such as protecting from market disruption or attracting talent. At the team/stakeholder level it might be removing stress or empowering financial independence. And at the personal level it might be helping to make life better for others or setting an example for one's children.

Considering these multiple levels of purpose can help individuals and teams to make connections between what they're doing and broader impact to provide added motivation to break status quo inertia and make change. And by sharing these *whys* as a group, people discover common ground, develop more empathy, and establish mutual understanding and trust.

How to find your why:

Step 1: Think about a potential change and why it matters. Write down your *whys* for each of the three levels:

- Why are the changes important to the organization (or to society as a whole)?

- Why are the changes important to the team (or to customers or to another stakeholder group)?

- Why are the changes important to you personally?

Step 2: Share your reflections with the group and discuss:

- Are there common themes among your own whys or with others?

- What aspects of this particularly resonated with you and with others as you shared your stories?

Step 3: Seek ways to amplify your whys in what you do and in how you communicate.

NOTES:

References

1. "Lighthouse Project: A Baby Saving Innovation—The Embrace Infant Warmer." EFCNI (26 June 2018). https://www.efcni.org/news/lighthouse-project-a-baby-saving-innovation-the-embrace-infant-warmer/.
2. Kelly, Eamonn, and Jason Girzadas. "Leading Through an Age of Discontinuity." Deloitte (2022). chrome-extension://efaidnbmnnnibpcajpcglclefindmkaj/https://www2.deloitte.com/content/dam/Deloitte/us/Documents/about-deloitte/us-leading-through-an-age-of-discontinuity.pdf.
3. Yamada, Makiko, Lucina Q. Uddin, Hidehiko Takahashi, Yasuyuki Kimura, Kazuya Takahata, Ririko Kousa, Yoko Ikoma, et al. "Superiority Illusion Arises from Resting-State Brain Networks Modulated by Dopamine." *Proceedings of the National Academy of Sciences of the Unites States of America* 110, no. 11 (12 March 2013): 4363–67. https://doi.org/10.1073/pnas.1221681110.
4. Edmondson, Amy C., and Zhike Lei. "Psychological Safety: The History, Renaissance, and Future of an Interpersonal Construct." *Annual Review of Organizational Psychology and Organizational Behavior* 1, no. 1 (21 March 2014): 23–43. https://doi.org/10.1146/annurev-orgpsych-031413-091305.
5. Vickberg, Suzanne. "Barriers to Breakthrough: Why Psychological Safety May Not Be Enough." Deloitte United States (13 March 2023). https://www2.deloitte.com/us/en/blog/business-chemistry/2023/barriers-to-breakthrough-why-psychological-safety-may-not-be-enough.html.
6. Grant, Adam. *Originals: How Non-Conformists Move the World.* Penguin Publishing Group, 2017.
7. Stavrova, Olga, and Ehlebracht, Daniel. "The Cynical Genius Illusion: Exploring and Debunking Lay Beliefs About Cynicism and Competence." *Personality and Social Psychology Bulletin* 45, no. 2 (2019): 254–69. https://doi.org/10.1177/0146167218783195.
8. Grant. *Originals.*
9. Black, David. "Being Creative with a Bear and Honey." Dtinblack (26 May 2018). http://dtinblack.github.io/creative-solutions/.
10. Hewlett, Sylvia Ann, Melinda Marshall, and Laura Sherbin. "How Diversity Can Drive Innovation." *Harvard Business Review* (2013). https://hbr.org/2013/12/how-diversity-can-drive-innovation.
11. Christfort, Kim, and Suzanne Vickberg. *Business Chemistry: Practical Magic for Crafting Powerful Work Relationships.* Wiley, 2018.
12. Christfort and Vickberg. *Business Chemistry.*
13. Firestone, Lisa. "Is Cynicism Ruining Your Life?" *Psychology Today* (3 December 2012). https://www.psychologytoday.com/us/blog/compassion-matters/201212/is-cynicism-ruining-your-life#:~:text=Many%20of%20our%20cynical%20emotions,we've%20turned%20on%20ourselves.
14. Krueger Jr., Norris, and Peter R. Dickson. "How Believing in Ourselves Increases Risk Taking: Perceived Self-Efficacy and Opportunity Recognition." *Decision Sciences* (May 1994). https://onlinelibrary.wiley.com/doi/abs/10.1111/j.1540-5915.1994.tb00810.x.
15. Ford, Henry. *Reader's Digest* 51 (September 1947): 64.

16. Abramson, Ashley. "Burnout and Stress Are Everywhere." *APA* 53, no. 1 (January 1 2022): 72. https://www.apa.org/monitor/2022/01/special-burnout-stress#:~:text=From%20longer%20work%20hours%20to,heightening%20everyone's%20risk%20of%20burnout.

17. Haas, Susan Biali. "3 Critical Signs of Burnout." *Psychology Today* (16 April 2018). https://www.psychologytoday.com/us/blog/prescriptions-life/201804/3-critical-signs-burnout.

18. Brennan, Dan. "Burnout: Symptoms and Signs." WebMD (3 December 2020). https://www.webmd.com/mental-health/burnout-symptoms-signs.

19. Vanderkam, Laura. "There's a Better Way to Reclaim Your Time Than 'Quiet Quitting.'" *New York Times* (13 September 2022). https://www.nytimes.com/2022/09/13/opinion/burnout-quiet-quitting.html.

20. "Awe Walk: Find Wonder and Inspiration Through a Simple Stroll." *Greater Good in Action*. University of California, Berkeley, 2023. https://ggia.berkeley.edu/practice/awe_walk.

21. Fisher, Jen, and Anh Nguyen Phillips. *Work Better Together: How to Cultivate Strong Relationships to Maximize Well-Being and Boost Bottom Lines*. McGraw-Hill Professional, 2021.

22. Moskowitz, Clara. "The Cosmological Constant Is Physics' Most Embarrassing Problem." *Scientific American* (1 February 2021). https://www.scientificamerican.com/article/the-cosmological-constant-is-physics-most-embarrassing-problem/.

23. Gilbert, Daniel. *Stumbling on Happiness*. Vintage Books, 2005.

24. Samuelson, William, and Richard Zeckhauser. "Status Quo Bias in Decision Making." *Journal of Risk and Uncertainty* 1, no. 1 (March 1988): 7–59. https://scholar.harvard.edu/files/rzeckhauser/files/status_quo_bias_in_decision_making.pdv.

25. Nickerson, Raymond. "Confirmation Bias: A Ubiquitous Phenomenon in Many Guises." *Review of General Psychology* 2, no. 2 (1 June 1998). https://journals.sagepub.com/doi/10.1037/1089-2680.2.2.175.

26. Ottati, Victor, Erika D. Price, Chase Wilson, and Nathanael Sumaktoyo. "When Self-Perceptions of Expertise Increase Close-Minded Cognition: The Earned Dogmatism Effect." *Journal of Experimental Social Psychology* 61 (November 2015): 131–38. https://www.sciencedirect.com/science/article/abs/pii/S0022103115001006.

27. Corbett, Martin. "From Law to Folklore: Work Stress and the Yerkes-Dodson Law." *Journal of Managerial Psychology* 30, no. 6 (2015): 741–52. https://doi.org/10.1108/JMP-03-2013-0085.

28. Muse, Lori A., Stanley G. Harris, and Hubert S. Field. "Has the Inverted-U Theory of Stress and Job Performance Had a Fair Test?" *Human Performance* 16 (1 October 2003): 349–64. doi:10.1207/S15327043HUP1604_2.

29. Brown, Paul. "The Failure Traps." *New York Times* (13 May 2006). https://www.nytimes.com/2006/05/13/business/13offline.html.

30. Christfort and Vickberg. *Business Chemistry*.

31. Vickberg, Suzanne, and Kim Christfort. "The Stress Study: Business Chemistry." Deloitte (2016). https://www2.deloitte.com/us/en/pages/consulting/articles/business-chemistry-and-stress.html.

32. Oakley, Barbara, and Olav Schewe. *Learn Like a Pro*. St. Martin's, 2021, pp. 13–22.

33. Amabile, Teresa, Constance Noonan Hadley, and Steven Kramer. "Creativity Under the Gun." *Harvard Business Review* (August 2002). https://hbr.org/2002/08/creativity-under-the-gun.

34. Sio, Ut Na, and Thomas Ormerod. "Does Incubation Enhance Problem Solving? A Meta-Analytic Review." *Psychology Bulletin* 135, no. 1 (January 2009): 94–120. doi:10.1037/a0014212.

35. Kaufman, Scott Barry. "The Emotions That Make Us More Creative." *Harvard Business Review* (August 2015). https://hbr.org/2015/08/the-emotions-that-make-us-more-creative.

36. Parker-Pope, Tara. "Strategies for Managing Food Cravings." *New York Times* (10 January 2022). https://www.nytimes.com/2022/01/10/well/eat/food-cravings-strategies.html.

37. Christfort and Vickberg. *Business Chemistry*.

38. Kapfhammer, Hans-Peter, Werner Fitz, Doreen Huppert, Eva Grill, and Thomas Brandt. "Visual Height Intolerance and Acrophobia: Distressing Partners for Life." *Journal of Neurology* 263, no. 10 (5 July 2016): 1946–53. https://doi.org/10.1007/s00415-016-8218-9.

39. Kahneman, Daniel, Jack Knetsch, and Richard Thaler. "Anomalies: The Endowment Effect, Loss Aversion, and Status Quo Bias." *Journal of Economic Perspectives* 5, no. 1 (Winter 1991): 193–206. https://www.aeaweb.org/articles?id=10.1257/jep.5.1.193.

40. Sirk, Christopher. "Fujifilm Found a Way to Innovate and Survive Digital. Why Didn't Kodak?" CRM.org (17 September 2020). https://crm.org/articles/fujifilm-found-a-way-to-innovate-and-survive-digital-why-didnt-kodak.

41. Klein, Christopher. "Why Coca-Cola's 'New Coke' Flopped." History.com (13 March 2020). https://www.history.com/news/why-coca-cola-new-coke-flopped#:~:text=To%20the%20shock%20of%20Coca,for%20its%20declining%20market%20share.

42. Kaufman, Scott Barry, and Carolyn Gregoire. *Wired to Create: Unraveling the Mysteries of the Creative Mind*. Tarcher Perigee, 2015.

43. Cell Press. "How the Brain Handles Surprise, Good and Bad." *ScienceDaily* (20 September 2007). www.sciencedaily.com/releases/2007/09/070919121557.htm; Suttie, Jill. "Why Humans Need Surprise." *Greater Good Magazine* (24 April 2015). https://greatergood.berkeley.edu/article/item/why_humans_need_surprise.

44. Cooper, Belle Beth. "Why Getting New Things Makes Us Feel So Good: Novelty and the Brain." Buffer (16 May 2013). https://buffer.com/resources/novelty-and-the-brain-how-to-learn-more-and-improve-your-memory/.

45. Sandlin, Destin. "The Backwards Brain Bicycle." *Smarter Every Day*, Ep. 133 (2016). https://www.youtube.com/watch?v=MFzDaBzBIL0.

46. Berg, Justin. "When Silver Is Gold: Forecasting the Potential Creativity of Initial Ideas." *Organizational Behavior and Human Decision Processes* 154 (September 2019: 96–117. https://www.gsb.stanford.edu/faculty-research/publications/when-silver-gold-forecasting-potential-creativity-initial-ideas.

47. Kotler, Steven. "The Science of Peak Human Performance." *Time Magazine* (30 April 2014). https://time.com/56809/the-science-of-peak-human-performance.

48. Huskey, Richard. "The Science of 'Flow States,' Explained by a Cognitive Science Researcher." Science Alert (5 January 2022). https://www.sciencealert.com/the-science-of-why-flow-states-feel-so-good-according-to-a-cognitive-scientist.

49. Gallego, A., L. McHugh, M. Penttonen, and R. Lappalainen. "Measuring Public Speaking Anxiety: Self-Report, Behavioral, and Physiological." *Behavior Modification* 46, no. 1 (2022): 782–98. https://doi.org/10.1177/0145445521994308.

50. Tajfel, Henri. "Social Psychology of Intergroup Relations." *Annual Review of Psychology* 33, no. 1 (31 December 1981): 1–39. https://doi.org/10.1146/annurev.ps.33.020182.000245.

51. Philips, Katherine. "How Diversity Makes Us Smarter." *Scientific American* (1 October 2014). https://www.scientificamerican.com/article/how-diversity-makes-us-smarter/; Reynolds, Alison, and David Lewis. "Teams Solve Problems Faster When They're More Cognitively Diverse." *Harvard Business Review* (30 March 2017). https://hbr.org/2017/03/teams-solve-problems-faster-when-theyre-more-cognitively-diverse; Rock, David, Heidi Grant, and Jacqui Grey. "Diverse Teams Feel Less Comfortable—and That's Why They Perform Better." *Harvard Business Review* (22 September 2016). https://hbr.org/2016/09/diverse-teams-feel-less-comfortable-and-thats-why-they-perform-better; Strauss, Karsten. "More Evidence That Company Diversity Leads to Better Profits." *Forbes* (25 January 2018). https://www.forbes.com/sites/karstenstrauss/2018/01/25/more-evidence-that-company-diversity-leads-to-better-profits/?sh=2914f5341bc7.

52. Johansson, Frans. *The Medici Effect*. Harvard Business School Press, 2004.

53. Amos, Jonathan. "Endurance: Shackleton's Lost Ship Is Found in Antarctic." *BBC News* (9 March 2022). https://www.bbc.com/news/science-environment-60662541.

54. Christfort and Vickberg. *Business Chemistry*.

55. Roller, Sarah. "Who Were the Crew of Shackleton's Endurance Expedition?" History Hit (n.d.). https://www.historyhit.com/the-crew-of-shackletons-endurance-expedition/.

56. Konrad, Alison, Vicki Kramer, and Sumru Erkut. "Critical Mass: The Impact of Three or More Women on Corporate Boards." *Organizational Dynamics* 37, no. 2 (April–June 2008): 145–64. https://doi.org/10.1016/j.orgdyn.2008.02.005.

57. "A Guide to Simpson's Diversity Index," Royal Geographical Society with IBG (15 December 2022). chrome-extension://efaidnbmnnnibpcajpcglclefindmkaj/https://www.rgs.org/CMSPages/GetFile.aspx?nodeguid=018f17c3-a1af-4c72-abf2-4cb0614da9f8&lang=en-GB.

58. Morrell, Margot, Stephanie Capparell, and Edward Shackleton. *Shackleton's Way: Leadership Lessons from the Great Antarctic Explorer*. Van Haren Publishing, 2002.

59. Nemeth, Charlan. *In Defense of Troublemakers: The Power of Dissent in Life and Business*. Basic Books, 2018.

60. Chamorro-Premuzic, Tomas. "Does Diversity Actually Increase Creativity?" *Harvard Business Review* (June 28, 2017). https://hbr.org/2017/06/does-diversity-actually-increase-creativity.

61. Mauran, Cecily. "Wise Life Advice from a 5-Year Old Is Going Viral on Twitter." Mashable (26 January 2022). https://mashable.com/article/twitter-thread-wise-life-advice-from-5-year-old-is-going-viral.

62. Yohino, Kenji, and Christie Smith. "Uncovering Talent: A New Model of Inclusion." Deloitte (2013). https://www2.deloitte.com/content/dam/Deloitte/us/Documents/about-deloitte/us-about-deloitte-uncovering-talent-a-new-model-of-inclusion.pdf.

63. Vickberg, Suzanne. "To Build Trust, Get Real." Deloitte United States (9 November 2020). https://www2.deloitte.com/us/en/blog/business-chemistry/2020/to-build-trust-get-real.html.

64. Yoshino, Kenij, David Glasgow, Joanne Stephane Heather McBride Leef, and Sameen Affaf. "Uncovering Culture." Deloitte (2023).

65. Yohino and Smith. "Uncovering Talent."

66. Stephane, Joanne, et al. "The Equity Imperative: The Need for Business to Take Bold Action Now." *The Equity Imperative.* Deloitte Development LLC (2021). https://www2.deloitte.com/us/en/pages/about-deloitte/articles/the-equity-imperative.html.

67. Christfort and Vickberg. *Business Chemistry.*

68. Cain, Susan. *Quiet: The Power of Introverts in a World That Can't Stop Talking.* Scribner, 2000.

69. Tulshyan, Ruchika, and Jodi-Ann Burey. "Stop Telling Women They Have Imposter Syndrome." *Harvard Business Review* (11 February 2021). https://hbr.org/2021/02/stop-telling-women-they-have-imposter-syndrome.

70. Kaufman, Scott Barry. "The Emotions That Make Us More Creative," *Harvard Business Review* (12 August 2015). https://hbr.org/2015/08/the-emotions-that-make-us-more-creative.

71. Marmolejo-Ramos, F., A. Murata, and K. Sasaki. "Your Face and Moves Seem Happier When I Smile." *Experimental Psychology* 67, no. 1 (2020): 14–22. doi:10.1027/1618-3169/a000470; Saunders, Elizabeth Grace. "How to Motivate Yourself to Do Things You Don't Want to Do." *Harvard Business Review* (21 December 2018). https://hbr.org/2018/12/how-to-motivate-yourself-to-do-things-you-dont-want-to-do; Brooks, Alison Wood. "Get Excited: Reappraising Pre-Performance Anxiety as Excitement." *Journal of Experimental Psychology: Genera*, 14, no. 3 (2014): 1144–58. https://doi.org/10.1037/a0035325.

72. Grant. *Originals.*

73. Ibarra, Herminia. "The Authenticity Paradox." *Harvard Business Review* (January–February 2015). https://hbr.org/2015/01/the-authenticity-paradox.

74. Patel, Alok, and Stephanie Plowman. "The Increasing Importance of a Best Friend at Work." Gallup (17 August 2022). https://www.gallup.com/workplace/397058/increasing-importance-best-friend-work.aspx.

75. Yohino and Smith. "Uncovering Talent."

76. Dweck, Carol. *Mindset: Changing the Way You Think To Fulfill Your Potential.* Random House, 2006; Amabile, Teresa M. "How to Kill Creativity." *Harvard Business Review* (September–October, 1998). https://hbr.org/1998/09/how-to-kill-creativity.

77. Coyle, Daniel. *The Talent Code.* Scribner, 2009.

78. Ward, Adrian F. "The Neuroscience of Everybody's Favorite Topic." *Scientific American* (16 July 2013). https://www.scientificamerican.com/article/the-neuroscience-of-everybody-favorite-topic-themselves/.

79. Patel, Jainish and Prittesh Patel. "Consequences of Repression of Emotion: Physical Health, Mental Health and General Well Being." *International Journal of Psychotherapy Practice and Research*, 1, no. 3 (2019): 16–21. https://doi.org/10.14302/issn.2574-612X.ijpr-18-2564

80. David, Susan. *Emotional Agility: Get Unstuck, Embrace Change, and Thrive in Work and Life*. Avery, 2016.
81. Kaufman, Scott Barry. "The Messy Minds of Creative People." *Scientific American* (24 December 2014). https://blogs.scientificamerican.com/beautiful-minds/the-messy-minds-of-creative-people/.
82. Redden, Joseph, and Ryan Rahinel. "Tidy Desk or Messy Desk? Each Has Its Benefits." *Association for Psychological Science* (6 August 2013). https://www.sciencedaily.com/releases/2013/08/130806091817.htm.
83. Dyson, Sir James. "Failure Doesn't Suck." Interview by Chuck Salter. Fast Company (1 May 2007). https://www.fastcompany.com/59549/failure-doesnt-suck.
84. Wujec, Tom. "Build a Tower, Build a Team." TED 2010, Brookline, MA. Video, 6:35 (2010). https://www.ted.com/talks/tom_wujec_build_a_tower_build_a_team?language=en.
85. Pennell, Kate Maria. "The Importance of Play in Creativity." Medium (24 September 2019). https://medium.com/swlh/the-importance-of-play-in-creativity-e284edbc6d93.
86. Brown, Stuart and Christopher Vaughan. *Play: How it Shapes the Brain, Opens the Imagination, and Invigorates the Soul*. Penguin Random House, 2009.
87. Guitard, Paulette, Francine Ferland, and Élisabeth Dutil. "Toward a Better Understanding of Playfulness in Adults." *Occupation Participation and Health* 25, no. 1 (31 December 2004): 9–22. https://doi.org/10.1177/153944920502500103.
88. Christfort, Kim. "The Cause Effect." Deloitte (2016). https://www2.deloitte.com/us/en/pages/operations/solutions/cause-effect.html.
89. Manson, Mark. "How to Get Motivated and Take Action," (n.d.). https://markmanson.net/how-to-get-motivated .
90. "Elephant in the Room," *Cambridge Academic Context Dictionary*. Cambridge University Press, 2009, p. 298. https://books.google.com/books?id=pqlRO2jdI2gC&pg=PA298&dq=#v=onepage&q&f=false.
91. Scott, Kim. *Radical Candor*.
92. Abi-Esber, Nicole, Jennifer Abel, Juliana Schroeder, and Francesca Gino. "'Just Letting You Know . . . ' Underestimating Others' Desire for Constructive Feedback." *Journal of Personality and Social Psychology* 123, no. 6 (24 March 2022): 1362–85. https://doi.org/10.1037/pspi0000393.
93. Farrell, D. "Exit, Voice, Loyalty and Neglect as Responses to Job Dissatisfaction: A Multidimensional Scaling Study." *Academy of Management Journal* 26, no. 4 (1983): 596–607. https://www.jstor.org/stable/255909.
94. Vickberg, Suzanne. "Barriers to Breakthrough: Why Psychological Safety May Not Be Enough." Deloitte United States (13 March 2023). https://www2.deloitte.com/us/en/blog/business-chemistry/2023/barriers-to-breakthrough-why-psychological-safety-may-not-be-enough.html.
95. Vickberg, Suzanne, and Melanie Langsett. "The Practical Magic of 'Thank You': How Your People Want to Be Recognized, for What, and by Whom." Deloitte (June 2019). https://www2.deloitte.com/content/dam/Deloitte/us/Documents/about-deloitte/us-about-deloitte-the-practical-magic-of-thank-you-june-2019.pdf.
96. Vickberg, Suzanne. "The Chemistry of Breakthrough Results." Deloitte United States (1 June 2020). https://www2.deloitte.com/us/en/blog/business-chemistry/2020/chemistry-breakthrough-results.html.

97. Kaufman, S. B., and E. Jauk. "Healthy Selfishness and Pathological Altruism: Measuring Two Paradoxical Forms of Selfishness." *Frontiers in Psychology* 11 (21 May 2020): 1006. doi:10.3389/fpsyg.2020.01006.

98. Le, Bonnie M., Emily A. Impett, Edward P. Lemay Jr., Amy Muise, and Francesca Gino. "Communal Motivation and Well-Being in Interpersonal Relationships: An Integrative Review and Meta-Analysis." *Psychological Bulletin* 144, no. 1 (2018): 1–25.

99. Haidt, Jonathan. *The Happiness Hypothesis: Ten Ways to Find Happiness and Meaning in Life*. Random House Business, 2021.

100. Divya, N. "Development of Creativity Through Heightening of Sensory Awareness." *ICoRD'15 – Research into Design Across Boundaries* 2 (24 December 2014), 63–73. https://doi.org/10.1007/978-81-322-2229-3_6.

101. Santos-Longhurst, Adrienne. "Everything You Need to Know About Sensory Deprivation Tank Therapy." Healthline (13 April 2020). https://www.healthline.com/health/sensory-deprivation-tank#TOC_TITLE_HDR_2.

102. Jonsson, Kristoffer, and Anette Kjellgren. "Curing the Sick and Creating Supermen – How Relaxation in Flotation Tanks Is Advertised on the Internet." *European Journal of Integrative Medicine* 6, no. 5 (October 2014): 601–9. https://doi.org/10.1016/j.eujim.2014.05.005.

103. Brown, Scott, and Alick Crossley. "Theater Review: The Freakily Immersive Experience of Sleep No More." Vulture (25 July 2018). https://www.vulture.com/2011/04/theater_review_the_freakily_im.html#_ga=2.164955711.1442886803.1670451730-1619401711.1670451729.

104. Butler, Anthony. "Improving Innovative Thinking Using This One Mental Trick." SDP/SI (2 August 2019). https://info.designatronics.com/blog/the-secret-to-engineering-better-solutions-practicing-unconscious-thought-theory.

105. Jung, Rex E., Brittany S. Mead, Jessica Carrasco, and Ranee A. Flores. "The Structure of Creative Cognition in the Human Brain." *Frontiers in Human Neuroscience* 7 (8 July 2013). https://doi.org/10.3389/fnhum.2013.00330.

106. Subramaniam, Karuna, J. Kounios, T. B. Parrish, and M. Jung-Beeman. "A Brain Mechanism for Facilitation of Insight by Positive Affect." *Journal of Cognitive Neuroscience* 21, no. 3 (21 March 2009). https://direct.mit.edu/jocn/article/21/3/415/4666/A-Brain-Mechanism-for-Facilitation-of-Insight-by.

107. Kudrowitz, B. M. "Haha and Aha!: Creativity, Idea Generation, Improvisational Humor, and Product Design." DSpace@MIT (2010). http://dspace.mit.edu/handle/1721.1/61610.

108. Sombatpoonsiri, Janjira. "To Defy a Dictator, Send in the Clowns." Zócalo Public Square (3 October 2017). https://www.zocalopublicsquare.org/2017/02/08/defy-dictator-send-clowns/ideas/nexus/.

109. Kim, K.H. "Playfulness: The Key to Creativity and Innovation." Idea to Value (19 May 2017). https://www.ideatovalue.com/crea/khkim/2017/05/playfulness-key-creativity-innovation/.

110. Aaker, Jennifer, and Naomi Bagdonas. (2017). *Humor, Seriously*. University of Chicago Press, 2017.

111. Milosevic, Yvonne. "Why What You Wear Affects Your Behavior—the Blacklight." The Blacklight (3 February 2021). https://theblacklight.co/2021/02/04/enclothed-cognition/.

112. Eadicicco, Lisa. "Laurene Powell Jobs Says People Have Been Misinterpreting One of Steve Jobs' Most Famous Quotes for Years." *Business Insider* (28 February 2020). https://www.businessinsider.com/steve-jobs-famous-quote-misunderstood-laurene-powell-2020-2#:~:text=Jobs%20said%20the%20famous%20line,Microsoft%20co%2Dfounder%20Bill%20Gates.

113. Gelles, David. "Laurene Powell Jobs Is Putting Her Own Dent in the Universe." *New York Times* (27 February 2020). https://www.nytimes.com/2020/02/27/business/laurene-powell-jobs-corner-office.html.

114. Snell, Jason. "Steve Jobs: Making a Dent in the Universe." *Macworld* (6 January 2023). https://www.macworld.com/article/214642/steve-jobs-making-a-dent-in-the-universe.html.

115. Kahneman, Daniel, and Amos Tversky. "Prospect Theory: An Analysis of Decision Under Risk." *The Econometric Society* 47, no. 1 (March 1979). https://www.jstor.org/stable/1914185.

116. Grant. *Originals*.

117. "I Have Gotten a Lot of Results! I Know Several Thousand Things That Won't Work." Quote Investigator. (31 July 2012). https://quoteinvestigator.com/2012/07/31/edison-lot-results/.

118. Farquhar, Brodie. "Wolf Reintroduction Changes Ecosystem in Yellowstone." Yellowstone National Park (1 July 2021). https://www.yellowstonepark.com/things-to-do/wildlife/wolf-reintroduction-changes-ecosystem/.

119. Eiseley, Loren C. *The Star Thrower*. Crown, 1978.

120. Mandela, Nelson. "One of the Most Difficult Things Is Not to Change Society—But to Change Yourself." African Ephemera Collection (n.d.). https://collections.libraries.indiana.edu/africancollections/items/show/8286.

121. Harrison, Scott, and Lisa Sweetingham. *Thirst: A Story of Redemption, Compassion, and a Mission to Bring Clean Water to the World*. Crown, 2018.

122. Aziz, Afdhel. "Charity: Water Announces Bitcoin Water Trust Reaches 100 BTC, Thanks to Matching Donation from Cameron and Tyler Winklevoss." *Forbes* (6 December 2021). https://www.forbes.com/sites/afdhelaziz/2021/12/06/charitywater-announces-bitcoin-water-trust-reaches-100-btc-thanks-to-matching-donation-from-cameron-and-tyler-winklevoss/?sh=45b129a5bf1d.

123. Sagan, Carl. "Skeptical Scrutiny." Good Reads (n.d.). https://www.goodreads.com/quotes/136838-skeptical-scrutiny-is-the-means-in-both-science-and-religion.

124. Vera, Dusya, and Mary Crossan. "Improvisation and Innovative Performance in Teams." *Organization Science* 16, no. 3 (June 2005): 203–24. https://doi.org/10.1287/orsc.1050.0126.

125. Stanford University and Mia Primeau. "Your Powerful, Changeable Mindset." *Stanford Report* (16 September 2021). https://news.stanford.edu/report/2021/09/15/mindsets-clearing-lens-life/.

126. Maio, Alyssa. "How the Best Method Actors Prepare for Their Roles." Studio Binder (14 June 2020). https://www.studiobinder.com/blog/what-is-method-acting/.

127. Philippot, Pierre, Gaëtane Chapelle, and Sylvie Blairy. "Respiratory Feedback in the Generation of Emotion." *Cognition & Emotion* 16, no. 5 (1 August 2002): 605–27. https://doi.org/10.1080/02699930143000392; Nair, Shwetha, Mark Sagar, John J. Sollers, Nathan S. Consedine, and Elizabeth Broadbent. "Do Slumped and Upright

Postures Affect Stress Responses? A Randomized Trial." *Health Psychology* 34, no. 6 (1 June 2015): 632–41. https://doi.org/10.1037/hea0000146.

128. Wood, Patti. *Snap: Making the Most of First Impressions, Body Language, and Charisma*. St. Martin's Press, 2016.

129. Arora, Shikha Puri. "Movement Coach: How Posture Affects Your Thoughts and Emotions." *Free Press Journal* (27 January 2023). https://www.freepressjournal.in/weekend/movement-coach-how-posture-affects-your-thoughts-and-emotions.

130. De Gelder, Beatrice. "Why Bodies? Twelve Reasons for Including Bodily Expressions in Affective Neuroscience." *Philosophical Transactions of the Royal Society B* 364, no. 1535 (12 December 2009): 3475–84. https://doi.org/10.1098/rstb.2009.0190.

131. "Gunder Hagg, 85; Runner Set World Records in the 1940s." *Los Angeles Times* (4 March 2019). https://www.latimes.com/archives/la-xpm-2004-dec-01-me-passings1.2-story.html.

132. Taylor, Bill. "What Breaking the 4-Minute Mile Taught Us About the Limits of Conventional Thinking." *Harvard Business Review* (10 April 2018). https://hbr.org/2018/03/what-breaking-the-4-minute-mile-taught-us-about-the-limits-of-conventional-thinking.

133. Science of Running. "The Roger Bannister Effect: The Myth of the Psychological Breakthrough." *Science of Running* (16 May 2017). https://www.scienceofrunning.com/2017/05/the-roger-bannister-effect-the-myth-of-the-psychological-breakthrough.html?v=47e5dceea252.

134. "Functional Fixedness." *APA Dictionary of Psychology* (n.d.). https://dictionary.apa.org/functional-fixedness.

135. "Understanding Functional Fixedness and How It Influences Behavior." *Better Help* (24 January 2023). https://www.betterhelp.com/advice/psychologists/understanding-functional-fixedness-and-how-it-influences-behavior/.

136. "Understanding Functional Fixedness." Better Help.

137. Berger, Warren. *A More Beautiful Question: The Power of Inquiry to Spark Breakthrough Ideas*. Bloomsbury, 2014.

138. "Home." Right Question Institute (10 January 2023). https://rightquestion.org/.

139. Chamorro-Premuzic, Tomas. "Why Group Brainstorming Is a Waste of Time." *Harvard Business Review* (March 2015).

140. Grant, Adam. "Opinion | Why I Taught Myself to Procrastinate." *New York Times* (16 January 2016). https://www.nytimes.com/2016/01/17/opinion/sunday/why-i-taught-myself-to-procrastinate.html?_r=1.

141. Dennis, A. R., and M. L. Williams. "Electronic Brainstorming: Theory, Research, and Future Directions." In P. B. Paulus and B. A. Nijstad (Eds.), *Group Creativity: Innovation Through Collaboration*. Oxford University Press, 2003, pp. 160–78. https://doi.org/10.1093/acprof:oso/9780195147308.003.0008; Diehl, Michael, and Wolfgang Stroebe. "Productivity Loss in Idea-Generating Groups: Tracking Down the Blocking Effect." *Journal of Personality and Social Psychology* 61, no. 3 (September 1991): 392–403. https://doi.org/10.1037/0022-3514.61.3.392.

142. Oakley and Schewe. *Learn Like a Pro*, pp. 13–22.

143. Nagji, Bansi. "Managing Your Innovation Portfolio." *Harvard Business Review* (24 February 2021). https://hbr.org/2012/05/managing-your-innovation-portfolio.

144. Tuff, Geoff. "The Innovation Ambition Matrix." *Managing Your Innovation Portfolio: Spotlight on Innovation for the 21st Century* (May 2012). https://www2.deloitte.com/us/en/pages/strategy/articles/managing-your-innovation-portfolio.html.

145. Katz, Fred. "Best Signature Moves in NBA History: Shooting Guards." *Bleacher Report* (27 September 2017). https://bleacherreport.com/articles/2370786-best-signature-moves-in-nba-history-shooting-guards.

146. Sunstein, Cass R., and Reid Hastie. "Making Dumb Groups Smarter." *Harvard Business Publishing Education* (1 December 2014). https://hbsp.harvard.edu/product/R1412F-PDF-ENG.

147. Rock, David, Heidi Grant, and Jacqui Grey. "Diverse Teams Feel Less Comfortable—and That's Why They Perform Better." *Harvard Business Review* (22 September 2016). https://hbr.org/2016/09/diverse-teams-feel-less-comfortable-and-thats-why-they-perform-better.

148. Armstrong, Jennifer. *Shipwreck at the Bottom of the World: The Extraordinary True Story of Shackleton and the* Endurance. Penguin Random House, 2000.

149. Rivera, Lauren A. "Hiring as Cultural Matching." *American Sociological Review* 77, no. 6 (28 November 2012): 999–1022. https://doi.org/10.1177/0003122412463213.

150. Sunstein and Hastie. "Making Dumb Groups Smarter."

151. Luz Eckrich, Sofia. "Peaks and Valleys = Values." Sofia Luz (blog) (20 February 2019). https://www.sofialuze.com/blog/2018/10/31/peaks-and-valleys-values.

152. Chapman, Gary. *The Five Love Languages: How to Express Heartfelt Commitment to Your Mate*. Northfield Publishing, 2005.

153. Brooks, Allison Wood, and Leslie K. John. "The Surprising Power of Questions." *Harvard Business Review* (May 2018). https://hbr.org/2018/05/the-surprising-power-of-questions.

154. Carnegie, Dale. *How to Win Friends & Influence People*. Simon & Schuster, 1936.

155. Colin, Chris, and Rob Baedeker. *What to Talk About: On a Plane, at a Cocktail Party, in a Tiny Elevator with Your Boss's Boss*. Chronicle Books, 2014.

156. Vickberg, Suzanne. "Build Trust with Your Ears." Deloitte United States (31 October 2022). https://www2.deloitte.com/us/en/blog/business-chemistry/2021/build-trust-with-your-ears.html.

157. Kreysa, Helene, Luise Kessler, and Stefan R. Schweinberger. "Direct Speaker Gaze Promotes Trust in Truth-Ambiguous Statements." *PLOS ONE* 11, no. 9 (19 September 2016): e0162291. https://doi.org/10.1371/journal.pone.0162291; Centorrino, Samuele, Elodie Djemai, Astrid Hopfensitz, Manfred Milinski, and Paul Seabright. "Honest Signaling in Trust Interactions: Smiles Rated as Genuine Induce Trust and Signal Higher Earning Opportunities." *Evolution and Human Behavior* 36, no. 1 (January 2015): 8–16. https://doi.org/10.1016/j.evolhumbehav.2014.08.001.

158. Wujec. "Build a Tower, Build a Team."

159. Tomac, Nikola, Radoslav Radonja, and Jasminka Bonato. "Analysis of Henry Ford's Contribution to Production and Management." *Pomorstvo* 33, no. 1 (27 June 2019): 33–45. https://doi.org/10.31217/p.33.1.4.

160. Mauzy, Jeffrey H. "Managing Personal Creativity." *Design Management Review* (9 June 2010). https://doi.org/10.1111/j.1948-7169.2006.tb00054.x.

161. Pinker, Steven. *The Stuff of Thought*. Penguin, 2023.

162. Weir, Kirsten. "Nurtured by Nature." American Psychology Association (1 April 2020). https://www.apa.org/monitor/2020/04/nurtured-nature.

163. Shapiro, Lawrence, and Shannon Spaulding, "Embodied Cognition." In Edward N. Zalta (Ed.), *The Stanford Encyclopedia of Philosophy* (Winter 2021). https://plato.stanford.edu/archives/win2021/entries/embodied-cognition/.

164. Vohs, Kathleen D., Joseph P. Redden, and Ryan Rahinel. "Physical Order Produces Healthy Choices, Generosity, and Conventionality, Whereas Disorder Produces Creativity." *Psychological Science* 24, no. 9 (1 August 2013): 1860–67. https://doi.org/10.1177/0956797613480186.

165. Andrade, Jackie. "What Does Doodling Do?" *Applied Cognitive Psychology* 24, no. 1 (31 December 2009): 100–06. https://doi.org/10.1002/acp.1561.

166. Clark, Timothy R. "To Foster Innovation, Cultivate a Culture of Intellectual Bravery." *Harvard Business Review* (13 October 2020). https://hbr.org/2020/10/to-foster-innovation-cultivate-a-culture-of-intellectual-bravery.

167. Doorley, Scott, Sarah Holcomb, Perry Klebahn, Kathryn Segovia, and Jeremy Utley. "Design Thinking Bootleg." PDF, Slide show. Hasso Plattner Institute of Design at Stanford University (n.d.). https://static1.squarespace.com/static/57c6b79629687fde090a0fdd/t/5b19b2f2aa4a99e99b26b6bb/1528410876119/dschool_bootleg_deck_2018_final_sm+%282%29.pdf.

168. Simon, Lauren S., Christopher C. Rosen, Ravi S. Gajendran, Sibel Ozgen, and Emily S. Corwin. "Pain or Gain? Understanding How Trait Empathy Impacts Leader Effectiveness Following the Provision of Negative Feedback." *Journal of Applied Psychology* 107, no. 2 (February 2022): 279–97. doi:10.1037/apl0000882.

169. Vickberg, Suzanne. "Barriers to Breakthrough: Why Psychological Safety May Not Be Enough." Deloitte United States (13 March 2023). https://www2.deloitte.com/us/en/blog/business-chemistry/2023/barriers-to-breakthrough-why-psychological-safety-may-not-be-enough.html.

170. Blunden, Hayley, Jaewon Yoon, Ariella S. Kristal, and Ashley Whillans. "Soliciting Advice Rather Than Feedback Yields More Developmental, Critical, and Actionable Input." *Harvard Business School Working Paper* no. 20-021 (August 2019) (Revised April 2021).

171. Shapiro and Spaulding, "Embodied Cognition."

172. Gibbs, Raymond W., and Wilson, Nicole L. "Bodily Action and Metaphorical Meaning." *Style* 36, no. 3 (2002): 524–40. http://www.jstor.org/stable/10.5325/style.36.3.524.

173. "Effect Of Colors: Blue Boosts Creativity, While Red Enhances Attention To Detail." University of British Columbia (6 February 2009). www.sciencedaily.com/releases/2009/02/090205142143.htm.

174. "Biophilic Design," EMEA United Kingdom (n.d.). https://www.interface.com/GB/en-GB/design/biophilic-design.html.

175. Ritter, Simone M., and Sam Ferguson. "Happy Creativity: Listening to Happy Music Facilitates Divergent Thinking." *PLOS ONE* 12, no. 9 (5 September 2017): e0182210. https://doi.org/10.1371/journal.pone.0182210.

176. Ozenc, Kursat, and Margaret Hagan. *Rituals for Work: 50 Ways to Create Engagement, Shared Purpose, and a Culture That Can Adapt to Change*. Wiley, 2019, pp. 6–8.

177. Thaler, Richard, and Cass Sunstein. Nudge: *Improving Decisions About Health, Wealth, and Happiness*. Penguin Books, 2009.

178. "Holborn Stand-Only Tube Escalator Trial 'Cut Congestion by 30%.'" *BBC News* (8 March 2017). https://www.bbc.com/news/uk-england-london-39206856.

179. Richarz, Allan. "The Amazing Psychology of Japanese Train Stations," Bloomberg (22 May 2018). https://www.citylab.com/transportation/2018/05/the-amazing-psychology-of-japanese-train-stations/560822.

180. Sinek, Simon. "How Great Leaders Inspire Action." TEDx Puget Sound, Seattle, Washington (2009). https://www.ted.com/talks/simon_sinek_how_great_leaders _inspire_action#t-255560.

Acknowledgments

It's not an exaggeration to say that this book would not exist were it not for our former teammate Ash Robinson speaking up one day and saying, "I think we need a manifesto" and then working with us to create one. For years we had been developing our Deloitte Greenhouse methodology for helping executives and their teams get to breakthrough, researching aspects of what we called the "science of experiential engagement," and building a database of methods to help individuals and groups innovate and make transformative change. But Ash's challenge to us was to codify that work into a clear articulation that would literally "make manifest" the principles underpinning our efforts and create a foundation to scale the impact of those principles across and beyond our team. So, before we recognize all the individuals who helped with the creation of this book, we'd first like to take a moment to acknowledge the work of Ash Robinson and of the other Deloitte Greenhouse teammates who helped to bring the Breakthrough Manifesto to life in the first place, including Kristin Pech, Jen Juneau, Naomi Bagdonas, Kate Tuscano, Rachel Keenan, Jen Veenstra, Judy Cheng, Sean Kelly, and Chris Ertel.

To all the members of the Deloitte Greenhouse past and present, as well as our broader Executive Accelerators ecosystem, thank you for living these principles out loud and for all you do to enrich our understanding of how and why they work for accelerating breakthrough.

There is truly an art to making a book look visually engaging, and we are indebted to Emily Hung Wilson for designing our cover and to Patricia Mozetic and Katie Wang for applying their artistic talent to creating the artwork inside the book, and under totally unreasonable timelines no-less. We're so grateful.

A book is huge a project, and at Deloitte we are lucky to have so many people who are experts at project wrangling, many of whom helped wangle this one. Special thanks goes to Zach Hughes, who went above and beyond to make this book great in many invisible ways, including reviewing and contributing to the manuscript, collecting stories from our teams, and helping us give proper credit where it's due by managing the massive effort of creating our reference section. Thanks as well to the many others who reviewed, commented, and contributed project management, expertise, and other efforts to this project, including Carrie Rodriguez, Tracy Timms, Katie Wang, Charmaine Stansall, Bec Heinrich, Em Havens, Kristin Chisesi, MaryBeth Neville, Tori Pylypec, Tony Scoles, Tarah Remy, Catherine King, Kristin Loughran, Kimmerly Cordes, Suzanne Nersessian, Heather McBride Leef, Kashmina Atwood, Michele Machalani, and Sameen Affaf.

We also tapped in the power of our Greenhouse teams in the US and globally to gather stories of how our methods have affected teams in the real world. Some of those stories appear in this book, and *all* of them have inspired what we've shared. Thank you to Rachiel Kennen, Jonathan Peterson, Amy Brenner, Elise McCormick, Jeff Metzler, Saagar Thakkar, Jeanne Strepacki, Taylor Beisell, Jennifer Juneau, Ajit Kambil, Sophi Martin, Summer Travis, Ellie Marsh, Bec Heinrich, Maggie Condon, Yo Daruwala, Emily Pearson, Javiera Echenique Berton, Tanya Shariff, Ricardo Cabello, Rodolfo Taboada, Catalina Gaitán, Cindy Loridon, Jen Hunter, Laura Baker, and Jeroen Huizer.

For help in making sure the world knows about and can benefit from this book—otherwise what's the point of writing it?—thank you to our colleagues Kristin Chisesi, Bridget Jackson, Whitney Ferguson, Nicole Pippert, Kori Green, and Jennifer Wotczak.

Thank you as well to the whole team at Wiley, especially Richard Narramore, Zachary Schisgal, and Michelle Hacker.

From Suzanne: I would like to thank my family and friends (and my dog, Lucy) for once again tolerating my absences and distractions as I worked to get this book out into the world. And most of all, thank you to Kim for continuing to inspire, coach, and spur me on to my own breakthroughs (even when I've said I couldn't possibly find the time or energy to write another book). I'm incredibly grateful for the opportunities I've had through working together, and I'm so appreciative of our partnership.

From Kim: I am so grateful to my husband, Jacob, and sons, Oliver and Alex, for their support, as well as to my parents, John and Gale, for reading through early drafts and offering their feedback. And of course huge thanks to Suzanne my coauthor now twice over. It's such a pleasure partnering with you, and I have enormous appreciation for your ability to identify and stay on top of all of the many details that are essential to our efforts coming to life. Ready to work together on book number 3? ☺

A Note from the Authors

First and foremost, thank you for diving in and opening yourself up to the world of breakthroughs! We hope you found inspiration from reading this book and are ready to obliterate, circumvent, or redefine the obstacles that stand between you and the outcomes you're trying to reach, or the person you are aiming to become. That you're ready to look for opportunities, seed fresh ideas, and cultivate positive action. That you're ready to breakthrough!

We also hope that this book becomes a companion on your breakthrough journey, and that you revisit it frequently to try out new methods or perhaps add techniques of your own. And should you crave more, we welcome you to check out a broader set of resources at BreakthroughManifesto.com to

- Uncover the underlying challenges blocking you from breakthrough
- Tackle those challenges with innovative methods, tools, and experiences
- Catalyze action to inspire positive change

Best of luck to you on your path to breakthrough, and we'd love to hear about your experiences and successes sparking transformative innovation.

Kim Christfort
linkedin.com/in/kimchristfort/

Suzanne Vickberg
linkedin.com/in/suzannevickberg/

Breakthrough Manifesto: Ten Principles to Spark Transformative Innovation
#BreakthroughManifesto | BreakthroughManifesto.com

The pursuit of breakthrough is often a team sport, and the teams most likely to get there are those who work across their differences to turn them into strengths. For more on how your team can do so, check out our companion book, ***Business Chemistry: Practical Magic for Crafting Powerful Work Relationships***, and the associated blog at ***businesschemistryblog.com.***

About the Authors

Kim Christfort

As the chief innovation leader for Deloitte's Executive Accelerators, I specialize in helping executives, teams, and organizations get to breakthroughs. Recognizing that companies are often held back not by technical challenges, but rather human ones, I've dedicated my career to exploring the intersection of human behavior, societal dynamics, emerging trends, and business strategy.

As part of this mission, I spearhead the Deloitte Greenhouse Experience, a group that diagnoses why groups get stuck, crafts methods to unlock opportunities, and designs and facilitates immersive team experiences to create lasting, positive impact.

These breakthrough experiences are typically engineered within six physical environments—permanent Deloitte Greenhouse spaces custom-designed to break teams away from "business as usual" with low- and high-tech elements geared to help senior executives grappling with adaptive challenges ranging from emerging marketplace disruption to organizational transformations.

I am also the architect and global leader of Deloitte's proprietary working style system Business Chemistry, used by more than 800,000 people around the world, coauthor of a *Harvard Business Review* cover story on Business Chemistry and of the book *Business Chemistry: Practical Magic for Crafting Powerful Work Relationships*. I am a frequent speaker, facilitator, and coach for global businesses.

Before taking on my current role, I spent 12 years in Deloitte Consulting specializing in customer and market strategy, and customer experience. Prior to that, I worked in public relations and marketing at The Benjamin Group Inc. I have an MBA from the Stanford Graduate School of Business, and a BA in science, technology, and society from Pomona College.

I live in California, where I enjoy time with family and friends, particularly outdoors in the state's lovely open spaces. I spend my free time painting, lyric writing, pursuing landscape projects, and creatively reusing and repurposing spaces, furniture, and household items, perhaps motivated by my unofficial role as "keeper of family junk no one can bear to discard."

Suzanne Vickberg

I'm a social-personality psychologist, a professional coach, and the chief researcher for the Deloitte Greenhouse. I'm intrigued by the many ways we can integrate empathy and creative problem-solving into our work, lives, and relationships. These are my favorite topics to research, and to think, talk, and write about.

In my current role, I help leaders and teams explore how their work is shaped by the mix of individuals making up the team and the unique characteristics they each possess. I guide them in creating cultures in which each member can thrive and contribute at their highest level. I'm also the primary author of the Business Chemistry blog (businesschemistryblog.com). My other books include *Business Chemistry: Practical Magic for Crafting Powerful Work Relationships* (coauthored with Kim Christfort) and *Divorce by Design: What If Staying or Leaving Aren't Your Only Options?*

Prior to joining Deloitte, I worked at the Great Place to Work Institute, Planned Parenthood Federation of America, and Mount Sinai School of Medicine. Along the way, I've earned a PhD in social-personality psychology from the Graduate Center of the City University of New York, as well as an MBA from the Stern School of Business at New York University. I am a trained professional coach, certified by the International Coaching Federation and the Coactive Training Institute.

Although I live in New Jersey now, I have strong Minnesota roots. When I can get to the woods, mountains, or a lake, those are my happy places. I'm an unapologetic introvert, so if I'm not out in nature, I'm probably on my sofa with my books, my space heater, and my dog, Lucy. Of course, I sometimes venture into the world of other humans to do something fun with my kids, hang out with friends, or volunteer in my community. Those moments bring me joy. So does arriving back home.

Index